P9-DCI-347

The TRUTH ABOUT DATING, LOVE & JUST BEING FRIENDS

and how NOT to be miserable as a TEENAGER because life is SHORT, and seriously, things don't MAGICALLY get BETTER after high school and lots of other IMPORTANT stuff, but we'll get to that later . . . CHAD EASTHAM

THOMAS NELSON
Since 1798

NASHVILLE   DALLAS   MEXICO CITY   RIO DE JANEIRO

To my father,
Thomas Kanada Eastham,
who is a good man.
Love you, Dad.

—Chad

© 2011 by Chad Eastham

All rights reserved. No portion of this book may be reproduced, stored in a retrieval system, or transmitted in any form or by any means—electronic, mechanical, photocopy, recording, scanning, or other—except for brief quotations in critical reviews or articles, without the prior written permission of the publisher.

Published in Nashville, Tennessee, by Thomas Nelson. Thomas Nelson is a registered trademark of Thomas Nelson, Inc.

Thomas Nelson, Inc., titles may be purchased in bulk for educational, business, fund-raising, or sales promotional use. For information, please e-mail SpecialMarkets@ThomasNelson.com.

Scripture quotations marked NIV are taken from HOLY BIBLE: NEW INTERNATIONAL VERSION®. © 1973, 1978, 1984 by International Bible Society. Used by permission of Zondervan Publishing House. All rights reserved.

Scripture quotations marked TLB are taken from The Living Bible. © 1971. Used by permission of Tyndale House Publishers, Inc., Wheaton, Illinois 60189. All rights reserved.

Page design by Mark L. Mabry

Library of Congress Cataloging-in-Publication Data

Eastham, Chad, 1980–
    The truth about dating, love & just being friends : and how not to be miserable as a teenager because life is short, and seriously, things don't magically get better after high school and lots of other important stuff, but we'll get to that later.../Chad Eastham.
        p. cm.
    Includes bibliographical references.
    ISBN 978-1-4003-1641-0 (pbk.)
    1. Dating (Social customs)—Juvenile literature. 2. Dating (Social customs)—Religious aspects—Christianity—Juvenile literature. 3. Teenagers—Juvenile literature. 4. Interpersonal relations in adolescence—Juvenile literature. I. Title. II. Title: Truth about dating, love and just being friends.
HQ801.E275 2011
241'.6765—dc22

                                                2010045088

Printed in the United States of America

11 12 13 14 15 16 RRD 6 5 4 3 2

CPSIA: Mfg. by RR Donnelley/Crawfordsville, IN/February 2011/PPO# 118084

CONTENTS

INTRODUCTION V

1. WHAT'S UP, MILLEYS? 1
2. DATING, FACTOIDS, AND QUARK-GLUON PLASMA 13
3. DUMB DATING MISTAKES—THAT EVEN
   SMART PEOPLE MAKE 34
4. WHAT TO EXPECT WHILE YOU'RE EXPECTING—
   A DATE 52
5. LOVE AND OTHER CHEMICAL IMBALANCES 65
6. JUST FRIENDS!?! 87
7. WHAT DO THEY WANT, ANYWAY? 109
8. CRAZY, DUMB, AND MIXED-UP FEELINGS 131
9. MISERABLE TEENAGERS 143
10. HAPPY TEENAGERS 167
11. IT'S NOT OKAY TO BE DUMB 188
12. THE PROBLEM WITH FALLING IN LOVE WITH
    MYTHICAL CREATURES 213
13. WHY THIS BOOK COULD BE STUPID 223
14. LOTS OF OTHER IMPORTANT STUFF THAT
    WE'RE FINALLY GETTING TO LATER 239

NOTES 243

Don't think you're
on the right road
just because it's a
well-beaten path.

—Author Unknown

INTRODUCTION

The Truth about Dating, Love & Just Being Friends...

and how NOT to be miserable as a TEENAGER because
life is SHORT, and seriously, things don't MAGICALLY
get BETTER after high school and lots of other
IMPORTANT stuff, but we'll get to that later . . .

Hi there, I'm Chad. It's great to meet you too. Well, I am just going to assume that it is great to meet you too. *And* . . . that you are super cool, and that you like me too, and that we become besties, and just talk and talk, and then laugh, and then you learn stuff, and everything becomes better because we are spending all this time together. Right? Right? You don't have to answer now . . . just get back to me later . . . maybe.

I suppose the first thing I should do is explain the title. I know, it's long, and it's a run-on sentence. But guess what? So are most of yours. Texting really is ruining your spelling, FYI. Moving on. Most of my writing comes from talking with teens and reviewing their questions. Mix that in with piles of research and a bunch of stats on young adults and teenagers, and I find some interesting stuff to talk about. Teens also write to me at . . . stuff@chadeastham.com, and I try to write back. It's amazing what you can learn from people's questions, stories, e-mails, letters, and conversations. And girls have lots, emphasis on *lots*, of questions. These are usually questions about dating, love, how to act around the opposite sex in general, being "just friends," and how to be happy. And guy's questions are . . . well . . . shorter, but still interesting. Now here's a letter I rarely see:

Chad,

You said in one of your books that you wished you got more e-mails from people saying how much they like themselves. Well, I just thought I'd send you an e-mail telling you that I like myself, and I feel "beautifully and wonderfully made." Thanks so much!

—Beth

Beth,

I really do wish I got more letters like this one. I'm pumped when I do. And I'm happy for you. I wish and hope that everyone could say those things confidently.

—Chad

It is a reality that there are some kids who feel this way. But unfortunately most don't. Have you ever thought about why some teens are so happy, and so many others aren't? I mean, really, why are some people so successful, smiley, laugh-prone, and optimistic while other people keep falling down, have broken relationships, become jaded and cynical, and see each period in their lives as bringing a little more cloud cover?

Is there an answer? Is it simple? Is it one of those magi-cal number tricks like "6.7 Things That All Happy, Successful People Do" or "11.1 Mistakes That All Losers Make"? Or are you like me, and you really get annoyed when people offer sim-ple answers to complex life situations? "Five Miraculous Secrets to Being Happy and Gorgeous and Perfect Forever!" Yeah.

Few things in life are that simple, but there are things that some people are doing, or not doing, that we can learn from. And guess what? Most of them start early! And a lot of them have to do with relationships. And not just romantic relation-ships, but all kinds of relationships in your life—parents, friends, teachers, boyfriends/girlfriends, the kid you meet at camp—you name it. The people in your life and how you interact with them can have a huge impact on whether or not you consider yourself "happy." Your behaviors and interactions with others are kind of like the seed of a tree. What kind of seed, where you plant it and when, the weather, and how it is tended will affect every-thing about the tree. Wow. Did I really just use a tree analogy? I'm sorry. I'll do better in the future.

Effort is only part of the equation when it comes to being happy. It's also the know-how and the tools that we choose to use. Maybe happy people do have some advantages. Maybe they have something figured out that other people haven't. Maybe they do certain things, have certain lifestyles, or don't do other things and that's the secret of their happiness. By looking at what happy people have in common, we may be able to learn their secrets.

What are some of the biggest issues in your life that you mea-sure your happiness by? What are the biggest relationship issues you're dealing with? You may be nothing like these teens, or exactly like these teens, but here are some typical questions that people send me.

Hey, Chad,

Question for you. Is it at all possible for a guy and a girl to be "just friends," or do guys and girls ALWAYS start to like each other??? A couple of girls won't stop talking about this, and I guess I don't know the answer either.

—Kevin

Chad-y-oo,

To put it bluntly, there is a guy that I kind of liked, but then he got weird. Doing stuff like grabbing my butt, touching places that should definitely not be touched in any way, trying to kiss me, and always getting close to me. At first, I liked the attention from him. Then, well, it got old—fast! I started to feel worthless, like I was being used like a toy. Only being there for his pleasure and fun. I tried to ignore him at school, but he thought it was a game and figured I was playing hard to get. Then, he would touch and hug me more. I wasn't able to stop him or push him away. I just gave up entirely. Now this is all in public and all quite embarrassing. I really don't know what to do whatsoever. Can you help me?

—Terri

Chad,

Help! I was with a guy for seven months, and it has been the worst roller-coaster ride and nightmare of my life. He didn't know what he wanted. One day he said he loved me, the next he loved me like a sister, or he wouldn't have any feelings toward me at all. He based love on a percentage with me. He would tell me he loved me 45 percent, or sometimes 30 percent, or maybe 57 percent, if I was lucky. I made some bad decisions, and we did the sexual stuff. Now he won't talk to me, and he acts like I don't exist.

I am broken.

—Erin

Chad,

So I really like this guy . . . we have tons of things in common . . . like he is the most AMAZING singer ever. I just always seem to be the "friend" and I don't know why . . . a lot of the time, I think it is something wrong with me, but my friends tell me otherwise . . . but what am I doing wrong? I have only liked 3 guys in my entire life . . . and I was always just the friend. Why are girls like me just the friend?

Thanks!!

—Abbey

In addition to these questions, there are lots of other important questions people your age ask. Questions like . . .

✓ What makes happy people happy?

✓ Why are lots of people miserable?

✓ When should I start dating?

✓ How do I know if someone likes me?

✓ Do girls care more than guys?

✓ Why do books and stories about vampires and teenage love do so well? (Don't get me started. Never mind, too late.)

We'll jump into these questions throughout the book. Or maybe we'll walk into them, if you prefer a more leisurely pace. Or skip maybe. Wait, do people still skip? I don't know if I want to. Your call. Just let me know. Either way, we're going to dig through some of these issues teens (and all people) deal with and try to get to the truth of them.

—Chad

WHAT'S UP, MILLEYS?

Do you know what large bird buries its head in the sand? The ostrich, right? No. Wrong. There has never been a single documented account of the largest bird in the world burying its head in the sand.

It was a guy named Pliny the Elder, a Roman historian, who most likely mistook his observation of the giant bird. What really happens is that the bird lies down on the ground, usually on its nest, and flattens its neck out, so that it can scan the horizon and look for predators. Pliny also thought that the ostrich could stare at its eggs with such intensity that it would make them hatch. Really, man? 'Cause that seems logical.[1]

So what's the point with the ostrich? The point is that we make all kinds of observations about all kinds of things. Some are right, some not so much. For example, people say things all the time about teens and their habits, opinions, and lifestyles. And they *love* to talk about how texting makes you dumb. Not true. It does, however, make you a horrible driver. So please . . . stop trying to kill pedestrians!

Although it's not good to text and drive, it is good to make observations. It can be helpful to know the habits of the people you are traveling through life with. Not so you can be like everyone else, but so you can at least know some of the things that make you a part of the group. Just keep an open mind and make *careful* observations. I mean, you don't want to be an ostrich trying to bury its head in the sand only to find out that you aren't supposed to do that. Mainly because you would suffocate, and you would be a bald bird.

▶▶ Traveling the Teen Highway

You may not know this about yourself, but right now you're on the road to somewhere. Do you know where you're going? No? Well, that could be a bad thing, but it's not necessarily. Being uncertain of where you are going doesn't make you lost. I mean, I guess it sometimes does, obviously. But not always. Sometimes it's okay to *not* know exactly where you are headed, at least not right away. This kind of represents your teen years in a lot of ways. You are figuring stuff out. You don't have to have it all "figured out" already. Big distinction. You are on a journey, and that is the adventure of it.

> Not all those
> who wander
> are lost.
>
> —J. R. R. Tolkien

On any journey, it's helpful to observe the other journeyers traveling with you. It would be sad to be hiking along in the woods for years and never see the fifty other people hiking along with you just a few feet away. Then one day you suddenly see them, and you're like, "Oh man, have you been out here the whole time? Seriously? We probably could have talked and shared some beef jerky or trail mix or something, you know. How did I not see you?"

It's sad when people do that. 'Cause it's fun to travel with others, especially when you are all on the same journey. So let's check out a few facts about your fellow life travelers.

A Snapshot of Your Generation

Maybe you hate computers. Maybe you love texting. Maybe you grew up in a religious and/or spiritual environment. Maybe you want to wait until you have seen Africa and Europe before you have children. Maybe you have kissed a lot of people or have even messed around. Maybe you just hold hands and are saving your first kiss until you are married. You could be a capitalistic, youth-group fanatic who loves Jesus and Republicans, or you could be a person who couldn't care less about politics. Maybe you love aardvarks. Get my drift? You could add twenty-five more categories of likes and dislikes, and you might be on either side of any of them. Either way, you simply fall into a very mixed bag of young people who have been born since the 1980s.

You are the Millennial Generation. Or as I sometimes like to call you, the *Milleys*. But I'm not great at nicknames.

And while you are unique and special—just like everyone else—there are a lot of things you and your peers may have in common, or not. So here is a little snapshot that describes some, only *some*, of you and the people in your "generation."

Sorry, You're Labeled

The Millennial Generation is meant to refer to those born from about 1980 until just after 2000. This means that you are the first generation of people who will become adults in a new millenium—the 2000s. The people before you are referred to as Generation X; they were born from 1965 to about 1980. Actually, I'm in the Millennial Generation with you, although I teeter on the edge of Generation X.

Before Generation X, we had the Baby Boomer Generation, which many of your parents fall into. Baby Boomers were born after World War II when everyone went on a baby-making crusade and moved to the suburbs. This was the age of the "white picket fence" and the mom who always had dinner ready for the family, which she cooked while wearing a dress and an apron. Not something you identify with much. Before that, there was the Silent Generation, which includes adults born from 1928 through 1945. The Silent Generation were the children of the Great Depression and World War II. Their title referred to their conformist views (that means just going along with the crowd) and their loyalty to politics. The Greatest Generation were the adults who fought in World War II, and the Lost Generation was the generation before that; they fought in World War I. So, you see, generations—like people—have different personalities. That's the simple way of saying it.[2]

Why is this important, Chad? I'm starting to get bored.

It's important because YOU, the Millennials, are creating your own personality as well. You are thought to be very expressive, more liberal than other generations, open to new ideas and change, and more confident and upbeat than other generations.

> Be open-minded,
> but not so open-
> minded that your
> brains fall out.
>
> —Stephen A. Kallis Jr.

And while you are more diverse, both in ethnicity and in culture than older adults, your generation is, in general, less religious. You are less likely than other generations to serve in the military. You are also on track to be the most educated generation in American history. Yippee, right? I mean, the access to information is not even comparable to what it was fifty years ago. What's up, Internet?

You are the first generation to have a full-on romantic relationship with your phones, computers, and any other media-based digital device that becomes the latest and greatest craze. You—both guys and girls—are much better at multitasking than any other generation in the history of the world. I mean, who has just an alarm clock by their bed? You have a phone with Internet access and an alarm clock on it. That way you can tell the time and make sure you are updated instantly if Jeff posts that he just watched a funny video on YouTube, and then you can call your best friend about it. Earth-shattering news like that can't wait more than three minutes to be told, after all.

> *You are the first generation to have a full-on romantic relationship with your phones, computers, and any other media-based digital device that becomes the latest and greatest craze.*

This also leads to a lifestyle of "convenience" habits that aren't always smart. Like driving and doing anything else while you're driving! More than two-thirds of teens admit to texting while driving. Just drive! You are going to kill someone! Don't hit my grandma; she's little!

Almost 83 percent of teens sleep with a phone next to them.[3]

Here are some more interesting and unique things about the people you're growing up with:

- More than 75 percent of teens have created a profile on a social networking site. Although most do still place privacy boundaries on their profiles. (Good idea, by the way.)

- One in five teens has posted a video of themselves online.

- Almost 40 percent of Millennials have a tattoo; 18 percent have six or more. I don't have one. Please make sure your parents don't yell at me as though

I said for you to go get a dragon tattoo or the
Chinese symbol for *tambourine*. Thanks.[4]

Technology Use for Teens

%. 87 percent of teens use the Internet.

%. 74 percent of teens who use the Internet also instant
message.

%. 81 percent of teens on the Internet play games online.

%. 43 percent of teens have bought things on the
Internet. (I do love Amazon.)

%. 20 percent of teens say the Internet is their primary
tool for communication.

%. 37 percent use instant messaging to say something
they *would not* or *could not* have said in person or over
the phone. (So not a good idea.)

%. 50 percent of teens have sent a message to a stranger.
(Also not a good idea.)[5]

Religion-ish-ness

On paper, you are the least religious American generation
ever known. About 25 percent of young people are unaffiliated
with any religion. However, not belonging does not necessarily mean you don't believe in God. Teens pray as often as older
generations did when they were teens. But today's teens seem
to want to understand God as he applies to their lives directly,
more than just understanding God and religion from a place of
theology.[6]

Parent Stuff

Roughly 60 percent of young people today were raised by both parents, which is a smaller percentage than other generations. But in contrast to that statistic, Milleys place marriage and parenthood above both financial and career success. That says something. But it doesn't say that you are in a hurry to get married. The average age of newlyweds is now over twenty-six years old, and that number is increasing slightly and will probably level off at around age thirty. The number of unmarried women who are having babies has also gone up. (Something that will have big implications for your kids one day.)[7]

The average age of newlyweds is now over twenty-six years old.

Emotional Items

About 20 percent of youth will experience depression sometime during their teenage years. Eating disorders are another common issue surrounding teens and young adults. Although a lot of attention is given to it, the incidence of eating disorders among girls is actually lower than you might think: anorexia is around 1 to 2 percent, although in a particular school or community the number can be much higher. Bulimia is estimated to affect 2 to 3 percent of young people. These lower percentages are good news for young people.[8]

The most beneficial thing people can do for the treatment of depression is to walk consistently. The benefits of walking and exercise are about twice as successful in alleviating the symptoms of depression as any drugs on the market. And walking is free and keeps you healthy.[9]

Attitudes on Dating and Sexual Activity

%. 47 percent of teens in grades nine through twelve have had sex. But the flip side of this statistic is often not reported. It means that about 53 percent of teens, or the majority, are *not* having sex.

%. Less than 10 percent of boys or girls have initiated sexual intercourse before age fourteen.

%. 66 percent of teens in grades nine through twelve said they were abstinent—and had been for at least three months prior to their answer.

%. Just over half of the fifteen- to nineteen-year-old group has had oral sex.

%. By age seventeen, a majority of teens said that intercourse is an accepted part of dating relationships. *However* . . . that is likely a reflection of their pessimism about relationships, given that more than 80 percent of girls and more than 65 percent of guys who have had sex say they regret it. That's the *vast* majority, by the way. Time to rethink the sex issue, huh? Don't worry; we will later.

%. It is also acceptable to be unattached—and a large majority of teens say that they don't place much significance on dating relationships.

% Teens age thirteen to fourteen (82 percent) are almost as likely as older teens (92 percent) to have had a boyfriend or girlfriend.

% Half of preteens and teens said their parents had never discussed how to say no to sex.

% About 50 percent of teens said their parents had never told them about sexually transmitted diseases.

% Teens who say they can talk to their parents about sex are actually less likely to engage in risky behaviors.[10]

City Bound

Something that is super interesting about the Millennial Generation is that you are increasingly less fearful of cities. So much so that you want to move back to them. For the first time since around the late 1940s, people are starting to flock back to the cities to live—even those people who are from small towns and midsized communities. Your generation is more inclined to see the metro-urban appeal of life after high school and college.

A lot of this has to do with the ability to travel more easily. Just getting from point A to point B is much easier compared to fifty years ago. But the traveling between cultures also comes much more easily to the Milley Generation. You are much more accepting of the different races and ethnic mixes that are more likely to be found in cities.[11]

I, personally, would like to have both an apartment in Manhattan and a farm somewhere out in nowhere. I like both sorts of places for different reasons. I don't have either of those places; I would just like to. What about you?

Help Me Help You ◀

All of these snapshots describe you in some way. Some describe who you *are*, and some of them describe who you *are not*. They are just snapshots of some of the habits of teens around you. Maybe your opinions about dating and love are completely different from anyone else's. But they might be something like one of these . . .

Chad,

I was reading your books, and I realized that I don't really care about dating at all. My girlfriends at school are obsessed with guys and sometimes I think I am supposed to be. But then I realized, "I just don't care." Now I'm focused on color guard and working on journal articles, because I really want to work in journalism one day. Boys schmoyz.

—DeDee

Chad,

I have been in love three times. It never works! I am sixteen years old. How do you know when you find love??? Seriously. Cuz it hurts when a girl breaks my heart and hurts me, but I always find myself there. You can't *not* love someone, cuz it's how we are made. How do I deal with this???

—Ryan

Or, you could paint an entirely unique picture of a person in your generation. And people do every day. Here's one I'm sure is unique. She is so unique that she speaks a language I can't even understand. I have read this letter more than twenty times, and every time it's like setting off a bomb in my brain!

Dear Chad,

I really need your help. My best friend's boyfriend is being really rude to his ex gf, who is also my best friend. And my old best friend was best friends with her ex-boyfriend before the boyfriend I'm talking about now. So he talks horrible things about her, and another girl who is an old friend of mine and cousin of the guy who my friend dated before, so it's even harder. I told him to stop because I don't let her talk horrible about him. I tried to talk to another friend who is friends with him but it's hard because he likes a girl who I got mad at and she doesn't like me, but is friends with my old best friend, but not my friend anymore. Cuz he did that to other people and it wasn't nice. So then he just said "ok then I won't talk at all" and left. He's going to tell his gf, which will then make her mad!

Help Me!!!

    —Amber

Yeah . . . soooooo good luck with that. Although I do think she managed to mix in more than half the topics from this book into one gigantic paragraph.

Like I said, we have some similarities, but we are all different.

DATING, FACTOIDS, AND QUARK-GLUON PLASMA

Do you know how many states of matter there are? Solid, liquid, and . . . ? Gas, right? Well, not exactly. You should also include plasma, superfluid, non-Newtonian fluids, supersolids, neutronium, quark-gluon plasma, fermionic condensate, Bose-Einstein condensate, and strange matter, along with others that are even more boring sounding.

Take non-Newtonian fluids, for example. They are liquids that turn solid when stress is applied. The military is designing jackets made of this fluid. Think about what that means. The jacket has this non-Newtonian liquid in it, but if someone shoots you, the impact of the bullet on the liquid would make it solid and keep the holes out of your body. This practically laughs in the face of physics.

Or imagine this: a pool is filled with this liquid, so that it looks like a giant tub of white paint. If you stepped slowly into it, you would sink and end up covered with this slimy, wet goo. But if you were to run onto it, or jump onto it and start jogging around, you wouldn't sink. With the added friction and weight, the fluid becomes harder, almost like a glossy, thick Play-Doh, and you can walk right across it, without ever getting any on you. That pool already exists, by the way. You can even look it up on YouTube. Weird, but fascinating![1]

▶▶ It's Complicated

Sometimes there are things that are more complex than we have been led to believe. Like the states of matter. And like dating. For example, how would you answer this letter?

Hey, Chad!!!

I've just come back from a church camp where I made a lot of new friends, including guy friends. I've actually been going out with this guy for eight months already, and he doesn't really have a commitment to his faith as much as I do. And meeting new people who do, well . . . made me feel like we don't belong together. I really do love him, but now I feel like I just love him as a friend. I really don't know how to tell him gently, and I was wondering if I can have some advice. I also kinda developed a crush on one of the guys from camp, but I want to get to know him more before anything happens. Can you tell me how? Thanks again!!!

—Betsy

> *Sometimes there are things that are more complex than we have been led to believe.*

This is a good question. How would you answer it? And does your answer work for everyone? Is your answer based on your experience, or just your opinion? I also like Betsy's question because it brings to light a lot more questions, like . . .

- What does "going out for eight months" look like?

- How can you tell "friend" feelings from "romantic" feelings?

- How do people with different views of God work out their relationship?

- How do you break up with someone and not turn him or her off to what you say you believe about God?

- Why do some people get crushes on more than one person at once? Is that right, wrong, healthy, or what?

Let's pump the brakes on all the questions for a minute and start with an even more basic question, like, "Where does dating even come from?"

The History of Dating ◀

Please Stop Capturing Me!

At many points in our early history, there was no dating. In fact, if you were a girl, you would simply be captured. Men would often raid a neighboring village and take the women as wives, skipping the whole dating thing altogether, which probably made it less than enjoyable around the family dinner table.

DAD: What was everyone's high point for today?
MOM: Not being enslaved. Oh wait, I am a slave. Never mind.

Because the former husbands or brothers of the women who were captured often came looking for them, the women would be forced into a cave with their new husbands and hidden there throughout a full phase of the moon while being given a brew called *metheglin*, which is made from honey. Combine the moon and the honey drink and bam, new term. Thus, *honeymoon*. Sounds like a blast. Maybe it should have been called honey-*kidnapping*.[2]

Let's Get Medieval

Later, once people got out of the caves, and honor and chastity were held in higher regard in most of Europe, a guy would impress a girl by opening doors for her—rather than just grabbing her and dragging her through the door and off to a cave. Much better for conversation. Kind of shows that when society emphasizes certain behaviors, the people tend to fall in line with them. But while there was some wooing and courting, marriages were usually arranged by the parents.[3]

People Named Victoria

During the Victorian Era (1837–1901)—which oddly enough was named after Queen Victoria—people started viewing romantic love as a requirement for people to marry. Before that time, marriage more often happened out of a sense of duty or legality. Once romantic love became more of a requirement, though, people lightened up a bit and started spending more leisure time together before they decided if they wanted to get married. But there were still a lot of rules.[4]

If a boy wanted to speak to a girl in public or, say, walk her home, he would have to be introduced to her formally. Then he would present his card to her, kind of a school ID, so to speak. If she wanted him to walk her home, she would let him know by presenting her own card back to him. And if the parents were okay with it, the young couple could sit on the porch and spend time talking. In other words, there were still boundaries, and the girl could be choosy about whom she spent time with. This is why guys would try to make a favorable impression, something we still try to do now, even though sometimes we guys can do odd things that may or may not actually impress the girl.[5]

Odd Ways to Say "I Like You"

◎ In Nordic countries, single girls would wear a belt with an empty sheath attached. If a boy liked her and she liked him back, he would give her a big knife and she would wear it around proudly.

◎ Wanna go on an awkward date? In eighteenth-century Europe and America, a guy might go over to a girl's house to hang out and talk and get to know one another. But because he had probably worked all day, it was usually later in the evening. So they would be put to bed, fully clothed, with a "bundling board" between them so they couldn't touch. Sometimes the girl was even tied into a kind of sack. Bundling allowed the couple to talk and get to know one another but kept them from the unsafe urges of making out or doing other stuff. They probably talked about how awkward it was to be tied up. That would be on my mind.

In parts of Europe, if a guy liked a girl, he would send her a pair of gloves. If she wore the gloves to church, it was a signal that she liked him back and that they were kind of "going out." Call it the football jersey of England.[6]

Now Let's Be Pilgrimy

In the Colonial Americas, from the 1600s through the 1800s, dating was considered a luxury. If you lived back then, you wouldn't have time to do much more than make meals or work in the fields. Free time was hard to find. And dating requires quite a bit of free time. I'm sure *some* kids would go hang out in their horse carts in the evening and play games on their iPhones, but I couldn't find any historical accounts of that. So dating was done mostly to get married and have kids to help with all the work. 'Cause carving civilization out of the wilderness apparently involves a lot of work.[7]

How the Dating Game ◀ Got Its Start

Here is how and why "dating" began. Within the last hundred or two hundred years in "civilized" countries, if two young people wanted to spend time together, they would usually do this at the girl's family home. You would basically start dating with supervision. Not totally unlike today in some ways. That is, *if* you were from a well-to-do family. But if you were from a middle- or lower-class family who couldn't afford a home nice enough or big enough to invite people to, then you would spend time together in public.

If you think about it, you see how we still do some of the same things today. For example, you like someone. So you ask her out to do something in a public place. It's less pressure. You don't have the means to entertain her at your house with fancy dining and butlers, so you do something inexpensive to get to know one another. This is basically how dating started.

Dating is a broad term. *Courting* is kind of dating but generally has greater restrictions on alone time and physical contact, and it has more of a focus on preparing to get married as opposed to "just dating." Some people believe that courting helps people to not struggle with the same things they always have, like sex before marriage. Sex causes children (just in case you didn't know). And if you aren't married and get pregnant, especially if you are a teenager, life suddenly gets harder. Courting—as opposed to dating—is thought to help prevent that. However, in the 1770s—when the culture primarily "courted"—premarital pregnancies in the United States reached as high as 30 percent. Which is high. In other words, people back then were still struggling with and trying to figure out the same things we are now. So was courting causing the problem back then? Is dating the problem now?

No, it is a people problem. Courting doesn't mean that you will understand relationships any better; it simply is a different set of rules about how to have relationships.[8]

Dating has changed a lot over the centuries. I think getting rid of that whole capturing-people-and-hiding-them-in-caves thing is significant progress. The more we look at the past, the more we understand where we are. Then maybe we can know where to go in the future.

⏩ 5 Things You Should Know about Dating

1. Dating won't lead you to marriage.

Well . . . at least it won't when you are a teen. Because less than 4 percent of relationships end up in marriage, you might take note that even though people *feel* as if they will be with someone forever, the statistics tell a different story. It's better that you know ahead of time that your teenage relationships probably aren't going to last forever. It won't make things worse by knowing this; it can actually help a lot.

2. Dating should be fun.

Yet how many people do you know who suffer in relationships? Dating is supposed to be the easy part. It's meant to get to know one another. If dating isn't easy, then I promise you that marriage with that person will most likely be miserable. As a Christian, I believe that relationships are designed by God to help us complement one another and grow closer to him; therefore, dating should be a positive experience. If it isn't, you should reconsider how you date and whom you are dating.

3. Dating is an evaluation tool.

I'm not trying to kill romantic feelings. However, some people are guided through their dating *only* by their feelings, and that's usually a recipe for disaster. Dating is your opportunity to evaluate other people and how well they fit with you on many levels. Used properly, it will make the rest of your life better. Used improperly, it can be a bomb.

4. Dating is not a replacement for living.

Any well-balanced person knows that dating and relationships are an important part of life, but they aren't supposed to be ALL of your life. Oftentimes people become enamored with their relationships and forget about everything else. Dating is meant to add dimension to your maturing life, not to replace everything else in it. Plus, sooner or later you'll find that dating really won't replace everything else anyway, and you'll end up crying, and I would prefer that didn't happen.

5. Dating, or not dating, is your decision.

To be honest, although I am writing about all this dating stuff, in some ways I never really cared that much about it. I always liked having friends, but the thought of having a girlfriend or spending a bunch of time dating people seemed exhausting to me. I felt that I wanted to do a lot of other things with my free time. And to be honest, it didn't seem as though people who were dating or in relationships were any better off than I was. They usually seemed pretty stressed. Some people think dating is really important, and others don't put much time and effort into it. Either way, it's your decision. Don't feel pressured to jump into dating. It will come in the right time, and in the right ways, for everyone. It comes down to a personal decision. Oh, and your parents' approval. Legally, I agree with whatever they say.

➤ Photographs and Relationships

Has someone ever shown you a picture of something, but then they said that the picture didn't do justice to the real thing?

"She is so pretty, but this picture doesn't even show it."

"It's even better than the picture."

"It's even more amazing when you see it in real life."

Sound familiar? Pictures don't always capture the whole story. But sometimes pictures are actually better than the real thing.

I was looking online at some incredible photos of some of nature's most scenic places. A waterfall in Africa, the ocean view in the morning, peaks of mountains at sunset, lovey dovey, blah blah blah, neato pictures right? But after a little while, I kind of felt deceived. Here's why. One of those pictures was of a place that I had actually been to. It was up in the mountains. I had been out hiking for a couple days along a mountain ridge with a few peeps. It was some of the most incredibly striking scenery on our continent. When people see pictures of it, they always say, "I would love to go there!" But do you want to know a secret? Yeah, it was pretty. But it was also pretty miserable. Of course you can only know that once you have physically gone there. (Or you could choose to trust me, instead, and save yourself the trip and luggage fees. Totally your choice.)

So up on this mountain ridge, it was great. Amazing views!

Unbelievable scenery! And I'm glad I did it. But seriously—and I'm not kidding here—it was some of the grossest and nastiest back country you could ever step foot in. There were turds everywhere. And every kind of turd that you could think of. Cow, moose, duck, bear, fox, mosquito, fly—you name it, and it probably turded there. Did I mention the mosquitoes? Probably close to two thousand mosquitoes swarmed around me twenty-four hours a day. I probably ate at least two hundred of them. They do not taste like chicken. Then there was the mud, which would suddenly appear under the moss and suck my boot two feet under. And I had to constantly keep an eye out for bears. It was cold and super windy—so windy that the tent would blow over. Oh, and at 4:00 a.m., the sun was like a spotlight shining in my face. I guess I'm not sleeping. Nice.

But the pictures *look* great. So picturesque and peaceful. Like somewhere you would go to relax. But in reality it was one of the most unnerving places that planet Earth could offer you. So when I see pictures of pretty places, I also feel slightly lied to, because the reality of an experience is often different from the picture of an experience.

Now, Chad, how does this relate to dating? you ask. Dating can be like one of those pictures. It can be great. It can offer great views, a fun journey, and great memories. But if done without care, intelligence, and planning, it can also be treacherous. Some of you may already know that. So now let's try and take some clearer pictures of the reality of dating.

The reality of an experience is often different from the picture of an experience.

▶▶ What Is Dating?

Let's start with the basics. Some definitions. First define the term *house*.

House:

_____

Now, define the term *dating*.

Dating:

_____

One hundred people were asked to define these two words. For the word *house*, almost all of the answers looked similar:

✓ somewhere you live

✓ usually has four sides, a door, and windows

✓ made of wood or concrete, used for shelter

✓ a structure that humans build to accommodate people and their belongings

But when asked to define *dating*, their answers looked quite different:

✓ spending time with someone you like

✓ I dunno, it's different for everyone (problematic answer)

✓ a romantic relationship with someone of the opposite sex

✓ something that single people do (kind of obvious)

✓ a way to decide if you are getting married

✓ going places with another person to see if you like each other

✓ a girlfriend or a boyfriend hanging out

✓ when someone asks you out to something, and they have to pay for it

✓ what people do to feel better about themselves, or to see if other people like them

Notice anything different? There are a lot of different definitions of dating. That becomes a problem because if everyone has a different definition for dating, then how are people supposed to know how to do it, what works, and what to avoid? If people couldn't agree on the definition of a house, it would be a lot harder to build one. And if people don't know what dating really is and how to do it well, then they are more likely to run into trouble—which causes more confusion, more heartache, more misunderstanding, and takes away from something that can be fundamentally good.

If people couldn't agree on the definition of a house, it would be a lot harder to build one.

You can hate dating or love it. You can want to date a lot or never—it doesn't really matter. But either way, it will help if we all try to understand dating, and what is really underneath it. Turns out, there is a lot.

The Problem Isn't Dating

There are a lot of divided opinions on dating. Some people start dating at thirteen. Other people think dating is unnecessary and against their religious beliefs. Some will just float in and out of romantic encounters. Others will adopt terms like *courtship*, which is mostly a Christian term for dating intentionally for the purpose of marriage. Each group tries in its own way to avoid some of the problems associated with dating. But dating itself isn't the problem—it's all about *how* it's done. Before you can say how dating is done well, you have to define what in the world dating is in the first place.

So, Please, Define It Already

Dating is getting to know someone over an extended amount of time to determine if a romantic relationship is something worth pursuing.

Does that help? It's a simple definition, but it leaves some wiggle room because not everyone thinks about dating in the same way or does it for the exact same reasons. If you are dating someone, you are going to spend time with him or her. You are going to see if you like certain things about that person. You might also notice things that you don't like. Usually, if you like more things than you dislike, there's a better chance you will start to have feelings of endearment toward each other. Whether you do this in groups or in one-on-one time, you are sizing each other up to see if you enjoy the other person's company. Simple enough. But that's where the simplicity stops.

The Bad View

Try this:

Why do you think that dating could be bad?

_____

_____

_____

Here is where people often disagree. And oftentimes their faith or religious perspective can help shape people's opinion. So let's take the point of view for a second that dating isn't good and leads to bad things. Dr. Henry Cloud and Dr. John Townsend compiled a list of reasons why dating can be negative.[9] And plenty of people have told me why they think it's bad as well. Here are some of the objections:

- ✓ Dating creates heartache.

- ✓ People pick the wrong type of person.

- ✓ Dating leads to physical intimacy but not to commitment.

- ✓ Dating leads to pressure, mostly from guys to girls, to do things they aren't comfortable doing.

- ✓ Dating skips out on the friendship stages of relationships.

- ✓ Dating messes up your future marriage with someone else.

✓ People become sexually active because of dating.

✓ Dating causes people to replace love with physical relationships.

✓ Dating isolates people from other relationships.

✓ Dating distracts people from focusing on other things, like school, family, and sports.

✓ Dating creates a fake way for evaluating another person.

✓ Dating gets in the way of your relationship with God.

Wow! That's a pretty decent list. And you can easily see that, yes, some of these things are real problems. You should also know that the younger a person starts dating, the greater the risk that he or she will have a more negative encounter. I can't tell you how many girls and guys have told me they have dated since they were twelve years old. So they have never figured out anything about themselves as a single person first. In other words, the younger you start dating, the more you become distracted by it, and the worse you are at it.

The Good View 😃

Now try this:

Why do you think that dating is good?

_____

_____

_____

Did you notice something about the negative list earlier? Besides how negative it is? The reasons that dating really can be negative are a reality, but it's not because dating is the problem. For example, "dating leads to physical intimacy, but not to commitment." That's simply not true. For some, it is, sure. But plenty of people have dated someone and been able to keep their clothes on. And yes, dating does isolate some people from their friends. But I also know people who have become more socially active because they were spending time with someone who encouraged them.

> *Plenty of people have dated someone and been able to keep their clothes on.*

It's NOT Dating

Let's say that again: dating is *not* the problem. The problem is how we go about what we call "dating." It is kind of like cars. People get in car wrecks all the time. People lose their lives in car accidents. So are cars wrong? Are they evil? No. Cars themselves are not wrong; the problem usually happens because of the people who are driving them.

The same is true with dating. There is nothing inherently wrong with the concept of dating. It's a way for people to get to know one another. The problem happens with *how* we date, at what age we start dating, how we do it, the boundaries we place around it, how much of a priority we make it, and maybe most importantly, *why* we date.

Healthy people usually have better dating experiences than unhealthy people. Coincidence? No, of course not. If we grasp a healthy perspective of what dating is, we can see that there are benefits for people who choose to date well. Based on surveys and interviews I did with tenth through twelfth graders, and the research of Dr. Cloud, here are some of the reasons why dating can be beneficial:

1. Dating is natural.

There are certain biological truths. One of those is puberty. While growing up, you start to like people of the opposite sex. And if you are like me, you might believe that God and biology aren't separate things. Although dating is a pretty new trend in history, the desire to start looking around at the opposite sex, interacting with them, spending time with them, talking to them, and seeing what they think of you, has been taking place since the beginning of time and is a completely normal part of growing up.

2. Dating is a way to learn about yourself and others.

Granted, when you are thirteen, you don't need to really learn about yourself in romantic relationships. If you disagree, sorry, but you are wrong. When dating is done well, and in a safe environment, then it takes you to another level of understanding people and exploring the feelings that go beyond friendship. You need to know these things. Learning about them in safe situations with guidance from others is part of eventually moving away from the nest just as nature intends.

3. Dating helps build the skills you will need in relationships.

Whether it's talking about feelings, expressing concern, actively listening, finding out insecurities, or learning how to be honest, these are skills you need. Dating can be a place where these abilities start to develop. For example, listening. You will listen to a boyfriend or girlfriend in slightly different ways than you might an acquaintance. This takes practice. Or asserting yourself. I realized once I started dating that I had a hard time saying things in a straightforward way to someone of the opposite sex, especially if my opinion disagreed with a strong personality. In other words, I was in danger of letting myself be walked on. Realizing that helped me be aware of it and start to assert myself differently, which has helped a lot of my other relationships.

4. Dating can make you optimistic.

When you have fun with someone else, regardless of whether or not you continue down the romantic road, it makes you optimistic. For people who date without necessarily thinking they are going to marry the other person, it helps them evaluate the type of person they will want to marry in the future. Dating doesn't have to make people pessimistic about future relationships; it can also make them hopeful. As long as you keep your pants on.

5. Dating can teach you empathy.

Empathy is being able to place yourself in someone else's shoes. That's something God asks us to learn to do in life, in that he asks us to love people the way he loves them. To love other people, you have to be able to see things from their perspective. If dating is used to get to know other people, think about their stories, and learn about them, it can help you better understand other people and how to care for them as friends.

6. Dating helps you learn what you like and don't like.

Something sad that I have seen is this: Boy and Girl meet at college, sometimes a small Christian college. They've never dated before and haven't learned much about relationships. They start dating one another to get married. They strive to stay pure for the person they will one day marry, which is most likely the person they are now "courting," because otherwise it might be wrong to be in that relationship without the intention of getting married. Then they get married. A few years go by, and they start to wonder if they actually like the person they are married to. While this doesn't always happen, it does happen. When you date with your eyes open, you are free to evaluate the qualities that you appreciate about someone, as well as the qualities that don't work so well for you.

7. You can put dating in its proper place.

I've said this a thousand times: you probably won't marry the person you date in high school. In fact, there's a 96 percent chance that you won't. So if you assume your dating relationship won't last forever, you can view dating as an opportunity to learn about people, relationships, communication, and differences in personalities. If you don't jump into heavy emotions and you avoid the physical intimacy, then you will often find that dating can lead to great friendships. Then if the relationship continues, wonderful. And if it doesn't, you weren't counting on it to fulfill all of your needs anyway.

8. Dating is an important part of socialization.

At one time, homeschooled kids were stereotyped as socially awkward because they didn't get to experience a variety of social interactions. But there have been tons of innovations in how people homeschool. There are now homeschooling networks, sports leagues, trip-planning organizations, and lots of other socializing opportunities.

Similarly, dating can help you with socialization. It can help you learn how to interact in a variety of settings with a variety of people. It can help you learn to interact in groups, as well as one-on-one. Basically, it can help you deal with people better, because more than a few people share the planet with you.

9. Dating can give you a chance to practice self-control and caring.

Dating, done correctly, actually teaches you to use self-control. It can help you learn that when you think only about your needs, you are being selfish and you can hurt people. Just dating someone doesn't mean you will be led into temptation that you can't overcome. In fact, it can teach you to be more considerate and respectful of all people as well as set healthy boundaries for yourself.

Dating is not about a term; it's about people. And people can do things well or do them poorly. If they do things quickly and without thought, those things are usually done poorly. If they try to understand and plan ahead, they usually do much better. Dating is no exception.

There is no simple plan for dating that works for every single person. And there doesn't have to be. But it should be fun; don't forget that. What's important is that you take in all the facts, treat yourself and others with dignity, learn to value people, and realize that dating is meant to help us understand relationships in more ways than just kiss-i-ness and boyfriends or girlfriends. Although if you do date, keep those clothes on. Juuuust a thought.

DUMB DATING MISTAKES—
THAT EVEN SMART PEOPLE MAKE

Ever seen a beached whale? I have, but it was dead, and you could smell it from a mile away. Beached whales still confuse scientists; they really can't explain why it happens. Usually the whales die of dehydration, or they suffocate under their own weight. The weird part is, it's common for a beached whale to be dragged back out to deeper waters (say, by the people who are rescuing it) and then have the whale strand itself on the same beach again right away.

Some people speculate that because whales use the Earth's magnetic field to navigate, when the magnetic field is abnormal, they become disoriented. Other people believe that since whales use sonar, the sonar doesn't bounce off of a gradually sloped beach surface, and the whales can't tell the depth of the water until it's too late. Still others think that whales chase prey into shallow waters and simply get stuck by the tide.[1]

Either way, it's still sad. I mean, who hates whales? Not this guy. But it's also kind of dumb. If you live in the water, you should make sure you don't spend a lot of time outside of it. And whales are pretty smart. But smart animals and smart people do dumb things all the time.

I'm a moderately smart person, but I'm no genius—I'm sure of that. And for a smart person, I have done a lot of dumb things. In fact, a lot of people do really dumb things. I heard about one dumb story that blew my mind. Some people snuck into a ski resort and started climbing a mountain, planning on sledding down. Only thing is, they forgot the sled. So they took off one of the huge pads that goes around the base of the ski lift. The pad looked like a big green gym mat. They carried it all the way to the top of the mountain, and the first guy rode down on it. Ironically, he lost control (not that he had it anyway) and kept going faster and faster, all the way down the mountain on his mat-sled. Wouldn't you know it? He didn't live longer than the sledding experience. He ran straight into a giant pole at the bottom, the same pole that he took the pad off of, which now was not as soft when he hit it going forty miles an hour.

So like I said, smart people do dumb things all the time, and dating without the right boundaries and attitude is no exception.

Two things are infinite: the universe and human stupidity; and I'm not sure about the universe.

—Albert Einstein

▶ It Happens to the Best of Us

Being Desperate

It's unattractive. Simply put. But people do it all the time. It's the "Help me, I need to know if this guy [or girl] likes me, and he [or she] won't tell me, and I'm going crazy, and I don't know what to do!" kind of thing.

Dating isn't a game. But when you make it obvious how desperate you are for a boyfriend or a girlfriend, you are just asking for some unhealthy person to start playing games with your emotions. And the healthy people—the ones you do want to be around—will actually become less interested in you. Too many young people are kicking and screaming to be in a relationship. It is an obvious sign of immaturity, as well as a sign of how much they are looking to be loved by a peer because they may not be getting love from their parents or other people. Don't act desperate. There is no reason to. You can be an awesome person all by yourself. And when you figure out and pursue those things that make you uniquely you, that's when good relationships will start. Good relationships don't come out of desperation. Period.

> *Good relationships don't come out of desperation. Period.*

10 Things You Should NEVER Say to a Guy

1. **"Do you love me?"** When we figure that out, we'll let you know. Don't obligate or force the answer.

2. **"I just hate [fill in the blank] about myself."** Guys are fixers, but it's not a guy's job to fix you. Focus on the stuff you like about yourself more than the imperfections. He'll appreciate it.

3. **"Nothing's wrong."** Yeah, we know that there really is something wrong, but after two tries we're not going to beg you to tell us. If something is wrong, spit it out already.

4. **"Do you think she is pretty?"** That's a trap question, and we know it.

5. **"What are you thinking?"** It's hard for a lot of girls to understand this, but sometimes we really are just thinking about nothing. Accept what he tells you; it might be the truth.

6. **"Does this make me look fat?"** Seriously? This is a lose-lose question for guys. And no matter what we say, you'll either get mad or you'll think we're lying—or both.

7. **"My ex-boyfriend always. . . . "** Guys do have feelings, and that one can sting. Besides, if that other guy is so great, why is he your ex?

8. **"He said . . . and then she said . . . blah blah blah!"** You may not think it's gossip, but it is. And it makes guys wonder what you say about them when they're not around.

9. **"Do this! Don't do that!"** You can make requests and communicate with guys, but you aren't his mom. Don't act like it, and don't tell people what to do or not to do.

10. **"If you really cared about me, then. . . . "** Manipulation and guilt go both ways. These are those kinds of statements, and they don't do anyone any good in the long run.

People aren't Play-Doh, and you can't just go squishing them and trying to mold them.

Fixing People

Missionary dating, taming the bad boy, making the bad girl good. Whatever you want to call it, people often go into a relationship expecting to change the other person. It's more important to change and improve things about yourself and let that be naturally contagious. While opposites do attract, they can also destruct. Make sure you are dating someone because you enjoy who that person is, not because you think you can shape your date into who you want him or her to be. People aren't Play-Doh, and you can't just go squishing them and trying to mold them.

Expecting Mr. or Miss Perfect

You aren't perfect. Neither is anyone else. So don't expect them to be. It's okay to have high expectations. You should expect people to be encouraging, honest, and kind. But expecting them to be perfect is unreasonable, and it's about you pushing your own ideals onto others. It's selfish, unhealthy, and somewhat offensive. *Before* you start dating, sit down and realistically assess what character traits are negotiable (sense of humor maybe, sports, musical taste, physical looks, similar interests) and which ones are non-negotiable (respectful, honest, not a game player). Then you'll have a better idea of whether that little quirk in your date's personality is a real issue or not.

Feeling Sorry for Yourself

Having a bad day and wallowing in self-pity are two different things. Whether you're feeling sorry for yourself to get attention from other people or if it's because you aren't in a relationship, the result is the same. It sets you up for the habit of self-pity. And this doesn't bode well for any of your relationships.

Break out of that self-pity habit. Try new things. Get involved in something you haven't done before. Embrace being single and figuring out who you are as a person. Encourage other people to have their own lives. Fill your time up with the things and opportunities that you *do* have, not just what you *wish* you had. Oddly enough, this makes you more attractive, and you'll have a lot less time to feel sorry for yourself.

The Island of Yourself

While it's good to figure out who you are as a person, it's not good to just get stuck on yourself. People can become self-absorbed, which isn't good for relationships and isn't a very healthy place to be in general. If you have an "it's-all-about-me" focus, then you probably shouldn't be in a relationship right now. You need to get yourself back to a healthy place where you still consider your needs, but you also consider other people. Most people are extremely turned off by selfish behavior anyway. Remember a relationship is not just about what another person can provide for you; it's about how you can complement one another.

10 Great Ways Guys Turn Girls Off

While there are many more things that you probably should never do or say to a girl you are trying to impress—or possibly to any member of the human race—these ten spell *unsuccessful* more quickly.

1. **Make any sort of loud, bodily noise.** Burp-and-fart champions usually celebrate alone.

2. **Brag about your loud, bodily noise,** or compete with other guys in contests involving these musical notes. For whatever reason, girls just don't enjoy this. Go figure.

3. **Shove large quantities of food in your mouth and chew with your mouth open.** Compete with your buddies to see who can shove the most. Again, for whatever reason, this grosses girls out.

4. **Talk about how hot another girl is in front of your date.** If you really want to quickly deaden the relationship, compare her to the hot girl.

5. **Ask if she has gained weight.** Are you insane? I don't care if she has her own orbit—NEVER ask this.

6. **Talk only about yourself.** Quick way to fail. 'Nuff said.

7. **Say "I love you" when you don't really mean it.** It's dumb and it's mean.

8. **Pressure her, especially about sexual stuff.** If your sentence starts with "If you loved me . . ." then you're being manipulative—and a jerk.

9. **Be physically aggressive.** You are a male. You are larger and more intimidating to girls than you realize. When you get loud, angry, or physically aggressive, it naturally scares girls, and it won't do anything except make you seem scary and unstable.

10. **Criticize.** Girls are hard enough on themselves; they don't need your help. Try and keep it to a ten-to-one scale. Ten positive things for one thing that isn't. That's emotionally balanced.

Becoming Too Selfless

Being too selfless is like being selfish, but in reverse. Some people lose themselves in trying to care for and love other people. While considering other people is vital, losing yourself, your dignity, and your ability to draw boundaries can be harmful. Relationships always have a give and a get to them—make sure you aren't just giving all the time. One of two things usually happens to the selfless person: the other person either ends up becoming less interested or starts to use you like a box of Kleenex. Healthy people don't want to be in a relationship with someone who doesn't acknowledge his or her own needs. A healthy dating relationship will encourage you to become your own person and focus on your needs as well as the other person's.

Thinking Every Relationship Is "the One"

I'm not saying that God doesn't have just one person for you. I'm talking about getting fixated on the idea of finding the "one perfect person." You can place way too much pressure on yourself and others in the search for "the one." And you can start to get down on yourself if a relationship doesn't work out, because you're thinking that maybe you just blew it with "the one" and now you'll be alone and miserable forever! Don't do that.

Focus on finding people you enjoy being around, who complement your interests and personality. Relationships need to be built on respect and everyday habits, not just the galactic view that you have to be constantly searching for that one single person in the universe who is right for you. That is just *too* stressful, especially when you are young. When you focus on having healthy relationships, that is when you will find someone who is wonderful to be with. And that is the person who just might end up being "the one." Or not. And if not, because you've had a healthy relationship, you'll be better prepared when "the one" does come along.

Sassy, Rude People (AKA Annoying)

Teens can be outspoken and confident about expressing their opinions. That *can* be great, but it's not *always* great. There is a difference between expressing yourself and being rude and insensitive. Like it or not, rude and insensitive behavior is portrayed all the time in popular television shows. And because these people are always portrayed as getting what they want, teens can get the idea that rude behavior gets them what they want.

The real world doesn't work that way. Rude behavior gets you a lot less friends and a lot poorer quality of relationships. Good relationships, good friendships, and just about good anything are rooted in showing respect. When someone is blatantly rude, loud and controversial, shoving his or her counter-opinions down everyone's throat, the first thing I think isn't *Wow! What a confident person.* Instead, I usually think, *Wow! There are probably a lot of things going wrong in your life since you feel the need to act like this.*

Don't be rude. Mature, enjoyable people build others up; they don't tear them down. That's a good, basic building block for healthy communication so that you don't have miserable relationships. In case you wondered.

Good relationships, good friendships, and just about good anything are rooted in showing respect.

Dating with Your Eyes Closed

Chad,

There is a guy, and he is making my life torture. He tells me that he likes me and has feelings for me. Like when we are alone, he says I am special and that no other girl is like me and that he has these feelings that he can't describe. But when we are at school, or I see him any-where that other people are around, he treats me like I'm dirt. Do I not exist? Not to him I don't, I guess. Why would he say these things? I think that he does care for me and maybe loves me, but it's hard to tell when he does this. Please tell me what to do!

—Maggie

To Maggie, and all the other Maggies out there: This might sting, but I promised to be honest with you. Stop it! You have a brain, and it is not okay to be clueless anymore. Take a hint, open your eyes, and stop being delusional. Imagine your friend wrote to you and said the same thing. What would you say? Of course you would tell her that it's obvious that she is only dreaming— and the guy doesn't really like her. And it doesn't really matter *why*. You have to start looking at reality and not living in your own fantasy world, which can develop into a bad life habit.

Simple example. If someone walks up to me (Chad) and punches me in the face and says, "I love you," guess what? I'm probably going to say, "Oww." Right after that, I'm probably going to say, "I don't believe you."

Is someone hurting you with what they do and then saying "I like you" or "I care about you"? Because if someone is doing that, then it is now *your* problem. There are people who will appreciate you and people who won't. But it's up to you to decide if you will tolerate it or if you will learn to value yourself.

Take Maggie, for example. Maybe the guy does tell her and show her that he cares when they are together. That's a tough, mixed message to try to understand, and I feel bad for her. But it's also not the point. The point is that the guy—let's call him "Mikey"—doesn't get it, and neither does Maggie. Mikey doesn't love her or care about her, because his actions speak a lot more clearly than his words. If he were not sure how he felt that might be one thing, but to say he cares and then blatantly disrespect her around other people says he is hurting her and doesn't really care for her.

Please wake up. Please open your eyes. People aren't perfect. Sometimes they mess up. Sometimes they don't show care or love or affection or respect in the right ways. And probably neither do you. But even though this is true, you can still add up the facts and see if people are *showing you* that they care more than they are *saying* that they care. Focus on people's actions and not their words; it's a better pair of eyes to look through.

Being a Stalker

Don't! Just don't!

Stalkers don't usually think they are stalking, but everyone else does. There needs to be an equal amount of interest between two people. Anything too unequal and one person starts to act weird. Emotions get out of control. And there is nothing more unattractive to a healthy person than an unhealthy amount of fixation on another person or on a relationship. It will turn people away, and it will destroy your mind and emotions.

Ask someone you trust to help you look at your behavior. Search for balance. When people become obsessed and stalker-ish, there is always an imbalance in their lives.

Stalkers don't usually think they are stalking, but everyone else does.

▶▶ The Ultimate Dumb Dating Tragedy: Dating Violence

Dating violence is a real problem. It dehumanizes people, it devalues them, and it is so ridiculously hurtful and unnecessary.

My dad had a dog named Pepper. My stepmom and he rescued little Pepper when she was only about eight months old. She had been beaten and abused. They loved that little dog for about twelve years. For the first two years, she practically hid under the bed. It took longer than that before I could approach her without her shaking and freaking out. She eventually warmed up to people, but the rest of her life was affected by something that happened for only a fraction of her life. It always made us sad.

What makes me even sadder is when these things happen to human beings. And it happens a lot more than people realize. Statistics show that one in three teenagers has experienced violence in a dating relationship.[2] Violence happens when a person tries to control or maintain power over another person—which is fundamentally impossible and only creates destructive actions, feelings, and behaviors. Most of the victims of dating violence are young women, who are also at a higher risk for serious injury.

Statistics show that one in three teenagers has experienced violence in a dating relationship.

Teen Dating Violence Statistics

:(One in five dating couples report some type of violence in their relationship.

:(One in five college females will experience some form of dating violence.

:(A survey of five hundred young women, ages fifteen to twenty-four, found that 60 percent were currently involved in an ongoing abusive relationship.

:(One study found that 38 percent of date rape victims were young women from fourteen to seventeen years of age.

:(A survey of adolescent and college students revealed that date rape accounted for 67 percent of sexual assaults.

:(68 percent of young women who were raped knew their rapist either as a boyfriend, friend, or casual acquaintance.

:(Six out of ten rapes of young women occur in their own home or a friend or relative's home, not in a dark alley.

:(More than four in every ten incidents of domestic violence involves non-married persons.[3]

Although anyone can be a victim of dating violence, it's useful to note that victims of dating violence often have these characteristics in common:

:(They are inexperienced with how healthy relationships work.

:(They are looking for independence from parents and usually find someone rebellious to date.

:(They have an imbalanced view of what love should look like in a relationship.

:(They feel pressure from other peers to be in a relationship.[4]

The way people see themselves is also one of the indicators of potential violence. For guys, they usually:

:(feel they have a right to "control" other people.

:(believe that being physically aggressive is part of "masculinity."

:(believe that a partner is someone to "own" or "possess."

:(demand intimacy.

:(fear losing respect from other guys if they are supportive of or too influenced by their girlfriends.

:(were abused themselves.[5]

Girls who become victims often believe:

:(they can help or "cure" someone who shows signs of being abusive.

:(abuse is "normal" because they know others who are being abused.

:(they can't tell anyone or ask for help.

:(they did something to provoke their abusers to abuse them; it's their fault.

:(jealousy, possessiveness, and even violence show how much the abuser cares for them.

:(they have been abused by other people.[6]

It's important to choose your relationships carefully. But that's not enough. You have to learn to see and evaluate other people's behaviors ahead of time. Before you ever get into a relationship, decide for yourself how you expect to be treated and what you will not tolerate. You are too valuable to be treated without great dignity and respect—whether it's how you treat yourself or how you let other people treat you.

And although no one thinks that someone who likes them will abuse them, the truth is that it happens. Dating violence is most often done by a guy to a girl. But it can also happen to guys. Look for these early warning signs that someone might be an abuser, and consider them carefully:

:(extreme jealousy

:(controlling behavior

:(rush to get serious

:(mood swings

:(alcohol and drug use

:(explosive anger

:(isolating you from friends and family

:(being forceful during an argument

:(hypersensitivity

:(blaming others for their own problems or feelings

:(verbal abuse

:(a history of threatening other people[7]

No one deserves to be abused or threatened. Don't become another victim. And if you do find yourself in an abusive situation, help is out there for you. Check out the National Teen Dating Abuse Helpline at www.loveisrespect.org or 1-866-33-9474.

The Simple Truth about Dating

Dating can be a blast and a really important part of your life. It can also be stupid, and it can hurt people. Dating can help you grow as a person, or it can break you down. It can bring you into a closer relationship with God, or it can distract you from him. It all depends on *how* you date, the boundaries that you put around dating, *when* you start dating (the older the better, in every conceivable way), and *why* you decide to date in the first place.

It's your choice. It's up to you.

You aren't dumb. You are smart—now go and act like it.

4

WHAT TO EXPECT WHILE YOU'RE EXPECTING—A DATE

Do you know how to tell if someone likes you? You have a better chance of figuring it out by watching what he or she does instead of listening to what he says. If you want a date, you need to know if someone is interested. You can do this through body language. People do weird little things that they don't know they do.

For example, if someone likes you, he might direct his body and feet in a line pointing toward you. A guy might fix his shirt, hair, or tie. A girl will flick her hair more often, but only if the guy is in her line of vision or standing nearby. Then the eye games start. Smiling more often, even over a longer distance, is done to appear open and receptive to being approached. Smiling is the easiest signal to pick up. Eye contact builds strong attraction for two people who are interested. Her pupils may become larger, and she will tilt her head slightly while listening to you. Studies also show that people with mutual attraction will mirror one another's gestures as a way to build rapport with the person. So if a person is mirroring your movements or habits, it's a way to say that he or she likes you on some level. Subtle touches are also a telltale sign, although girls usually do this to convey friendliness and guys do it to show romantic interest. And the more correct posture and arching of the back and laughing that two people do, the more they are trying to say that they are interested.[1]

If these things all happen *before* you go on a date, imagine how complicated it can get after. It might be a good idea to have some expectations and understanding ahead of time. Ya know, in everything you do, but especially dating.

Are You Prepared?

Have you ever been completely unprepared? I have, and it doesn't make for a lot of fun. I took a group of freshmen into the mountains one summer. I didn't really have too much of a plan other than a couple days of hiking and camping. They knew to bring boots, a backpack, and a small list of items that had been spelled out to them. But there was a problem. A lot of them brought the wrong *types* of items from the list, and half of them brought new boots.

Important tip: don't ever do real hiking in new boots. Super bad decision for your feetsies. There will be blood.

This group of teens also came from sea level, and we were hiking up around twelve thousand feet. Things got ridiculous. Scary ridiculous. A few kids fell almost fifty feet off a cliff overhang when the rocks gave way. They didn't have any mountain experience, so they didn't know the rocks they were on would shift with weight. We thought they might have died, but they didn't. Just minor injuries—very miraculously, I might add. Also, kids were getting altitude sickness all the time. They were throwing up day and night. They would get dehydrated and need tons of water, which we didn't always have because we had to purify the water. Kids were out of shape and passing out all over the place. At one point, going up a thousand-foot steep hillside, I had a fifty-pound pack on my back and a chubby kid on top of that pack with another forty-pound pack on top of him. He had passed out and had to be carried. It was awful. Awful for the kids, and awful for me.

So basically, we weren't really prepared. And while it didn't kill us, it did leave a lot of the kids with a sour taste when it came to camping and hiking.

What about you? Do you have any idea what to expect? Are you prepared? Not just for hiking, but for the trek into the dating world? I don't want you to throw up and pass out on the journey. It will not make your date think well of you.

Start Simple

This is basic, but it's important. What do you expect when you are on a date? You don't have to know all the details of where and when, just what you expect to happen on a date. If you don't even think about it, how are you supposed to know what you want from a dating relationship? For instance:

✱ What manners do you expect from your date? Should he open doors for you? Should she pay for her own meal?

✱ Where will you go? What will you do? Will you be alone or in a group?

✱ What are your personal boundaries for kissing and touching?

✱ What will you talk about? What will you avoid talking about?

These are things you need to think about *before* you date. Because once you get in the middle of a date, it can be hard to think. Period. What are your thoughts on these questions about dating?

How much time do you spend together before you consider it dating?

_____

Do you have the same opinions as the other person? About God? About family and friends? About values? Is it important that you do?

_____

Do you consider dating an exclusive thing? Why?

_____

What happens when one person thinks you should date only one person at a time, but the other person disagrees?

_____

What do you think the point of dating is?

_____

Are you thinking about marriage when you start dating someone? Why or why not?

_____

Great—or Not So Great—Expectations

The whole point of these seemingly simple questions is to get you to use the prefrontal cortex of your brain—to make you think ahead. I want you to use your critical thinking skills to work out your own personal boundaries and expectations. So . . . let's think about it some more.

What do you expect from someone romantically?

_____

Is it right to expect anything romantic from someone who is fourteen, sixreen, or seventeen years old?

_____

If you believe you should be able to expect romantic things from other people, why?

_____

Do others have a right to expect anything romantic from you? Why or why not?

_____

Now: _Why?_ Have you thought about why you expect anything from other people, and where that comes from? Is it natural, is it biological, or is it because something is missing from your own family that you need? Are you not getting affirmed or loved in some way, so you reach out to other people to meet those needs? This is a pretty common pitfall that people don't look out for. But rest assured that those who don't have their eyes open to weird topics like this, often find themselves the victims of even weirder behavior.

Boundaries

It's all about boundaries. Boundaries are simply a way to give complicated things structure. You don't just go build a house. You draw it first: you give it distinct boundaries, walls, size, shape. It starts with a lot of thought. So do our relationships. So does dating. So do boundaries. And boundaries help build the structures of lasting relationships. *Before* you date, decide what boundaries you want to put on your relationship—both physical and emotional. It's just the smart thing to do. Here are a few boundaries you need to set for yourself before you begin to date:

 ✳ How much time are you going to spend together?

 ✳ How much time are you going to spend talking on the phone, texting, or chatting online?

 ✳ What physical boundaries have you set for yourself? What lines will you *not* cross under any circumstances?

 ✳ What kind of time will you spend with each other's friends and families?

These are just a few boundaries to have set for yourself before you let your heart get carried away in a relationship.

Questions That Just Won't Die

Some questions just won't go away. Year after year, they get asked more than any others. Even if people have different opinions on the answers, the questions themselves just keep getting asked.

Who should ask out whom?

Great question, because people won't shut up about what they think, which is actually pretty fun. Should the guy be the one to ask the girl out? Should the girl ask him out? Does it matter? Here are some quick responses from people:

* "What a stupid question!"

* "Who cares?"

* "What is this, the Middle Ages?"

* "Guys should always ask a girl out."

* "It doesn't matter when everyone texts anyway."

* "It doesn't matter who does the asking."

As you can see, the answers vary. But it's a great question because it brings up an important topic: does it make a difference—to guys or girls—who does the "pursuing"? Is the idea of a guy asking out the girl completely outdated?

So does it matter who does the asking? Yes, it does

matter. And it matters for reasons people don't always think of. Relationships tend to work out better when guys are the ones who initiate their intentions. You will often find that guys who don't have to work for anything or risk anything, also don't appreciate much of anything. If you want the simple truth, many guys will be flattered when a girl asks them out, but they will also be less interested. It's not that way for every single guy, but for most of us, it is that way. I have experienced it personally. I don't even like that I became less interested, but it wasn't something I ever felt I could control completely.

Don't get me wrong: at the end of the day, it is your choice. I am not trying to tell you what to do, and I am not saying that one way always works and the other way does not. Remember, girls can passively initiate a date too. In other words, the girl can let the guy know that he has a chance if he approaches her to ask for a date. You know, she can hint to a friend that she might be interested in the guy. The friend tells the guy, and then the guy gets up some nerve and approaches the girl. It's a natural game of cat and mouse. You may think it won't matter, but it does and here's why.

Guys need the exercise. No, really, they *really* do need to practice this. The question of who should do the asking is usually asked by girls because they are interested in a guy, but he is being hesitant, for whatever reason. But this isn't about girls. This is about a guy's confidence. You don't just *become* confident in life; you have to *practice* it. You have to swim into unfamiliar territory. You have to struggle before you can improve.

And guys have to learn confidence. Confidence is a muscle for guys, and they have to build up this muscle. One way they do this is to approach girls and show they are interested. By the way, being cocky isn't being confident. If you watch a guy try to impress a girl, and then watch him approach her honestly and ask if she would like to spend time together doing something nice that she would enjoy, you will see two different characters. Being cocky is a mask for being insecure. Being confident takes risk. There's a difference. A big difference.

So the next time you hear people talk about this question, remember, the question isn't about a rule; it's really about people.

How do you know if someone is really interested in you?

Chad,

There's this guy, and I can't tell if he likes me. Sometimes he completely acts like he does, and then other times I can't tell at all and it seems like he doesn't even know I'm alive.

—Jodi

I get a lot of variations of that letter—from both girls and guys.

Short answer: They should tell you. And they should be *able* to tell you. If they can't, then they either don't "like you like that," or they aren't old enough to be in relationships that say this type of thing. Having said that, there are some signs you can look for.

5 Ways to Know If He/She Is Really into You

1. The guy or girl tells you. Kind of a given.

2. They show up around you more. There's a good chance they are feeling things out.

3. They are respectful of your thoughts and feelings. And they intentionally seek out talking to you and asking you questions that are *actually* about you.

4. They are interested in the things that interest you. Finding common interests is good.

5. They don't play games with your feelings. This shows respect and confidence and intention. It also means they are using their actions to show that they care.

What's the best age to start dating?

Well, for starters, what do you think? Would you tell a six-year-old to date? No, that's a super weird thought. So is it fourteen, sixteen, eighteen, never?

The simple answer is this: I see nothing good coming from dating before the age of sixteen. That's my educated guess, along with the opinions of people who try to formulate weird math equations like that. In our culture, sixteen signifies more growth, responsibility, and personal freedom. But again, it's really something that you and your parents have to agree upon. I will give you this warning flag: the younger people are when they start dating, the more negative their dating relationships can be. The longer you wait to begin dating, the likelier you are to have focused on defining yourself, your personality, and your values. And in one of those weird, full-circle kinds of ways, you become a more attractive person. Now, I'm simply going to warn you: if one more thirteen-year-old comes up to me and says, "I have had a bunch of bad relationships and my question is . . . ," then I might break the nearest object that can be thrown. The world is full of things to do besides fixating on dating. It's an important subject in life, but still only one subject.

> *The longer you wait to begin dating, the likelier you are to have focused on defining yourself, your personality, and your values.*

Is dating an overall good thing or a bad thing for teenagers?

Overall, it *could* be good, but mostly it looks to be more negative than positive. Don't blame me. That's just what the evidence suggests. But as I said before, the problem isn't usually with dating. The problem is partly age, but it's also *how* people do it. If you place great boundaries and realistic expectations on dating, I think it can be good. But even with that said, I don't think that there are many things you'll learn from dating in high school that you couldn't learn just from having good friendships. Friends will help you learn a lot of the same relationship skills that you would learn from boyfriends or girlfriends—but usually in much less drama-filled ways.

Another pitfall of teen dating is that for many people it has a tendency to create some pain, or mistrust, or unrealistic views of relationships. In other words, baggage. Although there are ways to keep this from happening, choosing to postpone dating for a while probably won't kill you either. Just a thought.

But as I said earlier, I want you to use your own prefrontal lobe. Tap your forehead near your hairline. That's pretty close to where it is. What do you think? Take a look at the relationships around you, and make your own list of the benefits and drawbacks of teen dating.

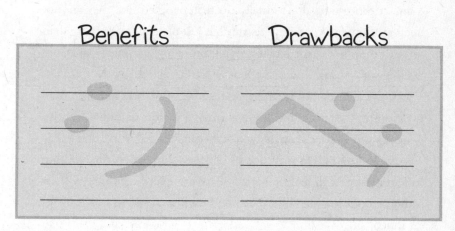

Benefits

Drawbacks

Why don't guys seem to care as much as girls?

It's not that guys don't care; it's that *people* don't always care. Sometimes they don't know how, and sometimes they just develop really bad habits. Sometimes those habits are being mean, inconsiderate, or selfish. Maybe they weren't taught how to care, because they didn't have caring parents. Perhaps they try to care, but they just need to learn how to do it well.

It's also not accurate to say that girls care "more" than guys. Guys do care, and oftentimes as much as girls; they simply express things in different ways. And sometimes girls are the ones who are mean, inconsiderate, or selfish. Then guys are the ones asking, "Why do I seem to care about this girl when she is just mean to me and doesn't seem like she cares about me?"

I'm not kidding. Guys really do ask that. And you would be surprised at how often they ask that.

Guys and girls generally express their feelings in different ways. Most of what guys are feeling happens internally rather than externally, especially at the onset of feelings. Girls are more likely to express themselves verbally, with body language, and with eye contact. Since guys don't usually do that, people think they are not feeling as much. Not true. The music is just playing inside more than outside. Another factor is that girls are more likely to start expressing feelings of care and endearment at an earlier age than guys.

Guys also tend to be more reserved about being in committed relationships. Bottom line, there is often a reason that they feel this way. It's a self-defense strategy. A guy can sense that he isn't ready for commitment. He may not be able to clearly explain why, but oftentimes he will feel hesitant and won't express himself with as much emotion as the other person; thus, it seems he is not "caring" as much.

Both guys and girls need to be wary of being one of those people who mistakes worrying, being insecure, and emotionally needy and clingy for caring. When you see these signs, it's often a huge hint that the person isn't ready for this level of relationship yet. And when you're young, you don't have to feel weird about that. It's pretty normal, and learning to care takes time and energy. Just don't underestimate how much guys do care, as long as you are paying attention to the right guys.

When you practice for the test ahead of time, you just do better. Even if you don't like that answer, you still know it's true. It's also true of your human tests and quizzes and relationships. I hope you will do some studying and show up for the dating test prepared. It won't be as stressful, and you'll just do better. Dating is a good thing. It's a people thing. You just have to do it wisely.

LOVE AND OTHER CHEMICAL IMBALANCES

Diamonds are a symbol of love. If a guy says "I love you" and gives a girl something with a diamond in it, it's probably more significant than if he high-fives her and shares his pizza. But do you know where diamonds come from?

Actually, volcanoes. Diamonds come from volcanoes, which makes them seem even better to me. They are formed two hundred to three hundred miles underground, inside a substance called *kimberlite* and are mined from areas where volcanic activity has taken place. Eruptions are what bring diamonds to the surface. They are more concentrated in certain geographical regions, such as South Africa, Australia, and Russia. The largest diamond isn't on Earth either. It's right above Australia, only eight light-years away. The diamond is inside the star Lucy in the constellation Centaurus and is roughly 2,500 miles across. It measures about ten billion trillion trillion carats. The star got its nickname from the Beatles' song "Lucy in the Sky with Diamonds."[1]

There is a lot to learn about diamonds. And if diamonds are one representation of love, then there is probably a lot to learn about love too.

I was in love once. Well, I mean for the first time . . . once. Well, actually it probably wasn't love. Now that I think about it, that makes no sense. I'll just tell you the story, and you can laugh at me. Better?

Once upon a time there was a boy who loved a girl, and her laughter was a question he wanted to spend his whole life answering.

—Nicole Krauss,
The History of Love

How on earth are you going to explain in terms of chemistry and physics so important a biological phenomenon as first love?

—Albert Einstein

First Love

I was just a budding flower in the spring of my youth, circa fourth grade. She was a blonde with a magical smile and beautiful braces. It almost hurt every time I saw her. Oh, the things we could talk about. I thought about all the ways I could make her laugh. She was incredibly personable and outgoing to be so young. She always looked good on camera. But Stacy (we were on a first-name basis in my mind), was really not responding to me the way that I had pictured. Our relationship was struggling. I think it had to do with my homework piling up. It also could have been because she was on TV, and we had never met in person. But I did have a lot of homework too.

Our relationship and my love was mostly one-sided, in that she had no idea I existed. This would later describe the entirety of my seventh-grade existence. But as for Stacy, she was the talented singer on *Kids Incorporated*, which I watched with anticipation every single Saturday. I was . . . ummm . . . *smitten* would be the correct term. Is *smitten* the shortened term for the smacking of kittens, you ask? No! Are you joking? Why would you even ask that? Who would hurt a kitten—are you crazy?

Okay, so I had never met Stacy. But she was the first girl who gave me strange feelings I couldn't explain. Feelings like I just wanted to see her again. Like I missed her when she went away. Like how grateful I was for basic cable. And here is the part where you can start making fun of me. I was so curious about her that I had to know more. I didn't have a lot of skills or resources in the fourth grade. But I did have a telephone. And I wasn't afraid to use it. (Remember, this was before the Internet boom, so my information about her was limited.)

I called the operator when my mom was at work and my sister wasn't around.

ME: Ummm, yes, operator? I am looking for my future girlfriend. You've probably seen her on TV. I mean, who hasn't? She sings good. She has an awesome headband and some cool jelly bracelets. She is older than me, but I plan on maturing pretty quickly, especially once I start getting some armpit hair. Anyway, could you connect me to her? [The operator, holding back her laughter, tried to help me a little.]

OPERATOR: Well, does she have a name?

ME: Her name is Stacy from *Kids Incorporated*.

OPERATOR: Well, do you know her last name or where she is located?

ME: Well, she is blonde, and she is on *Kids Incorporated*. Ummm . . . I can't remember her last name, but it starts with an *F*, and I'm gonna say that she is in New York, 'cause, I mean, she is on TV. So could you connect me now?

Unfortunately that day ended in tragedy—no phone conversation and no relationship. Mostly due to the operator laughing and hanging up.

It was sad. I guess I should have just said "Um, excuse me, operator, could you go ahead and shatter all of my dreams and plans for love today? Oh, you can? Fabulous. Really appreciate your time." What could have been, you know? If only things would have worked out.

Later, and I mean like ten or fifteen years later, I found out that the *F* was for Ferguson and that she had shortened her name to Fergie. She wasn't with *Kids Incorporated* anymore and had moved on to another music group having to do with black eyes and peas. What? Are you serious? My first love was Fergie?

When I realized this, I kind of felt embarrassed for a second. But then I compared my innocent young love to some of her later music, and let's just say it didn't feel quite the same. Oh, well.

It was completely weird realizing that Fergie was my first . . . love. Although we both know that "love" isn't really an accurate term. But it felt like it. Just like most people's first infatuation/love/crush/romance can take their feelings for a joy ride. Things get confusing, attitudes change, heart rates increase, short-term memory goes out the window, food loses its flavor, jealousy rears its ugly head, insecurities sprout up, and even just the scent of someone can send your brain scrambling.

Ahhh . . . love.

Love is a grave mental disease.

—Plato

▶ The Deep End of Love

Let's swim around in the deep end for a minute. Love is weird.
Most of our lives are fashioned and shaped around getting it and
giving it. When we are loved, life is better. If we are not loved,
or don't know that we are loved, or don't know how to be loved,
then our lives will center around trying to find love.

> *When we are loved,*
> *life is better.*

A lot of people don't feel loved, by the way. If you *do*
feel loved, then that is wonderful. But if you are like a lot of
other people, you may not feel deep down that you are loved.
I always knew that my parents loved me, but I didn't really
think that other people did. I mean, who cares if your parents
tell you that you're special if no one else does? At least that's
how I felt. So I felt unlovable. And when you feel unlovable,
it's as if you are a defective toy on the shelf. No one wants the
defective shelf toys.

Growing up, I felt awkward and out of place. Most people
feel that way at some point. But I felt like that at all points. So
I did what almost anyone else would do; I looked for accep-
tance, for love, for care, for affirmation that I was important.
Unfortunately, like many, I looked in a lot of the wrong places.

When you don't have the directions for how to do something right, you usually do it wrong. I know I did. It's as if you
would do anything to fit in. Hang out with anyone who seems
to accept you. Take almost any attention from the opposite sex

because it feels good. And all of these things just start a snowball of unhealthy behavior. Sorry to be your therapist about it. But I tried all the wrong ways, so I know these things.

A lack of love is at the center of bad boyfriends, bad girl-friends, teen pregnancy, heartache, drama, emotional torture, and staying in dumb or even dangerous relationships just to have one. It's not that people try to have these bad things; it's just that something needed is missing from their lives: love.

> *There is more hunger for love and appreciation in this world than for bread.*
>
> *—Mother Teresa*

Some people live their entire lives terrified that no one will love them. They act on these fears and try to control love. They search for it desperately. They try to force it or make it happen where it shouldn't. They can actually sabotage love because they won't let it grow naturally. People can lie to themselves in order to *feel* love.

Hi,

You write about love and talk about stuff like that. I
don't think anyone has ever loved me. I see people's
parents that love them, and it hurts inside because I
don't think I have ever had that. I do strange things,
and I try to get attention, and I think there is a lot
wrong with me. How am I ever supposed to be okay when
it feels like there is nothing about me that is wonderful, or worthy to love?

Amanda

Love is vital, and you have to have it. Without it, life suf-
fers. And if you don't have love—at home, from family, or from
friends—you have to be very careful about how you go looking
for love in a relationship. We'll talk more about that later. But for
now just know that people are not okay without love. Just as fish
need water, people need love.

▶▶ What Is Love, Anyway?

Here is how some people describe love. Note that these people,
although it's not their fault, are probably very wrong.

♥ A complete trust that your thoughts and feelings
and everything else in your life will be safe in the
hands of another.

♥ You can't do anything without thinking about him/her.

♥ Longing to hold—or be held by—that special someone.

♥ Wanting to be with him or her every second of the day.

♥ Without that special person, you feel incomplete and empty inside.

♥ The desire to learn everything about the one you love and to tell that person everything about yourself.

♥ Knowing that he or she will always be there for you no matter what happens.

♥ An intense devotion to a person.

♥ Knowing that nothing else matters more than the one you love.

♥ When you accept the other person entirely and completely.

♥ Knowing that if you were without that person, you could not live.

♥ Love makes you look down on everyone else,
   because they do not feel what you feel.

Here is another way to describe love. These are *way* more accurate.

♥ Love grows deeper and wider over time.

♥ Love is based in the best interest of someone else.

♥ Love is kind.

♥ Love is contagious and spreads more love and care
   to others.

♥ Love is patient.

♥ Love does not hurt, emotionally or physically.

♥ Love doesn't boast or brag.

♥ Love grows both people. It frees them and opens
   their hearts.

♥ Love embeds a deeper sense of trust and freedom,
   instead of fear and worry.

♥ Love is not jealous and does not create jealousy.

♥ Love is never selfish.

♥ Love is not rude.

♥ Love doesn't behave indecently.

♥ Love celebrates truth.

♥ Three things last forever: faith, hope, and love; but the greatest of these three is love.

> From the best-selling book on planet Earth,
> THE BIBLE, 1 Corinthians 13

Love is just a word, but is it a feeling, or is it a verb?

Feels a bit like Dr. Seuss maybe, but please stop thinking about love as just a feeling. Sure, love is a feeling in some ways. You can feel loved, and you can feel loving. But at some point the feeling of love has to be just one of many tools we use to understand love.

Chad,

Please help. I am sorry to bug you if you get this question all the time, but how do you know if someone really loves you? I am sixteen, and my boyfriend is seventeen, and we've been together for almost eight months. He says he loves me, and he tells me this all the time. He says I am his world, that he can't live without me. He says he will love me forever and always, and that he could never love anyone else as much as he loves me. I am confused sometimes because he gets so jealous, and sometimes he doesn't treat me the way that he says he feels about me. He still flirts with other people a lot, and his friends are terrible, and he makes less and less time for me. So I get confused. How do I know if he really loves me? This is confusing my heart.

—Aleesa

So as many times as I have said this to people, I'll gladly tell you again. An important way for you to learn about love is to stop thinking about love as simply a feeling and start looking at love as though it's a verb. A v-e-r-b. An action item. As in: Is what this person *doing* speaking louder than what he or she is *saying*?

> *Stop thinking about love as simply a feeling and start looking at love as though it's a verb.*

When people say they love something or someone, are they showing love more than they are saying love? Lip service is easier to do; showing love in your actions first is more honest and shows maturity. Don't fall for words if the actions are different. In other words, make sure someone isn't kicking dirt on you and saying "I love you" at the same time. Because only one of those things can be true. And I'm sure you can figure out which one if you look with your eyes open.

Actions before words, especially with words like *love*.

Read the Signs

Healthy Love	Not So Much
Relationship invites more people around it.	Shuts everyone else out; isolates and closes in.
The feelings are mutual.	One person feels romantic, and one person does not. It's a push-and-pull situation.
Conflicts are occasional, but when they occur, they promote growth.	Conflicts are frequent and create growing tension instead of growing resolution.
The other person's freedom and independence are important.	Freedom and independence create insecurity, controlling behavior, and conflict.
Desire is based on caring for the other person's well-being.	Desire is rooted in neediness and one's own desires.
The relationship is fun, and it makes life more enjoyable, easier, and pleasant.	The relationship is mostly work. It doesn't grow your belief that relationships are of more value than they are difficult.[2]

➡ 5 Top Tips on Finding True Love

1. Find a love role model.

It's been said that the best thing a dad can ever show his children is that he loves their mother. When you watch people do things correctly, it's a whole lot easier to get a good road map for yourself. After all, people usually repeat the behaviors they are surrounded by—positive or negative. You may have never seen love modeled in awesome ways, so you may need to do some searching. Are there any people you look up to, families or couples who are mature and seem to love one another in lasting ways? Look for love stories that are great, and take notes.

2. *Love* and *lust* are NOT the same thing.

They are related and they are often confused, but that doesn't make them the same thing. Let's not even call it lust. Let's call it physical desire, because that's what it is. And it's a natural part of life. But don't confuse intense physical or sexual feelings for love. And hey, trust me, it can be confusing. Just know the real measure of love goes beyond just sexual desire or physical attraction; instead, it's rooted in trust, commitment, and care.

3. Know that there are many types of love.

Love is most often associated with romantic love. But it can also take the form of familial love (your family), caring love (people in need), and friendly love, among others. Love is a big word, and it encompasses a lot. Make sure you don't simplify it to just the one form of romantic love. It would be a shame to limit what love is.

4. Let your definitions of love grow.

Whether it's princess what's-her-face with her Prince Charmy Smile or the little old man who visits his wife in the nursing home every day, even though she no longer remembers his name, love has many different definitions. What you think about love today is not what you thought five years ago, and it won't be the same ten years from now either. What you love in people now might change later. How you give love and receive it will also change. Just be open to the idea that your definition of love is limited to your experiences, and there are a lot more experiences yet to learn from.

5. Be an optimist.

Even if your heart has been broken, if you haven't yet experienced love, or if you just don't think much about it, you should still choose to be an optimist, to have a positive outlook. Those who look for the positive and believe in the best will find it. People tend to live out their fears, but they also tend to live out their hopes and dreams. So dream plenty. And when you think about and plan for what love might mean in your life, make sure those dreams and plans stay sunny.

You Might Not Be In Love If . . .

Sorry if it's sunny where you are, and I just brought my rain cloud over to play. But you should know that many times people are not in love, even though they think they are. They are in *infatuation*, and it is not the same thing. When you get completely smitten with someone, it's easy to confuse those romantic feelings with deep down love. Normally teens should have parents right there to help balance their lives and not let them obsess over just one person. But that doesn't seem to happen as often as it should, for a lot of reasons. Lots and lots and *lots* of you seem to be out there on your own. You are trying to figure out how to have relationships and trying to understand your own feelings, but with no one older and wiser helping you. Fact: You will confuse you.

Why, Chad? you ask.

Well, because what happens in your mind and body aren't just up to you. Your body and brain are going through all kinds of changes as part of growing up. And then infatuation causes even more changes in your brain. To put it bluntly, your brain goes a little psycho. Left to its own neurotic devices, and without proper boundaries and proper people, the brain of an infatuated person very much resembles that of a drug addict.

It's the feelings of love and the chemicals your brain produces (like dopamine and serotonin and oxytocin) that you become addicted to. Three areas of your brain, the right ventral tegmental region, the medial caudate nucleus, and the nucleus accumbens, start to go nuts. I know how pumped you are to learn these words. The combination of these three areas and the chemicals they produce works together to shorten your attention span, cause short-term memory loss, and impact your goal-oriented behavior. You get adrenaline rushes, your heart rate goes up, you can have trouble focusing, and you can fixate on thoughts of another person. In other words, your judgment becomes impaired. You can easily become distrusting, anxious, insecure, and overanalyzing. It's easy to see why people often feel overwhelmed by their feelings in a relationship.

*Left to its own neurotic devices, and without
proper boundaries and proper people, the
brain of an infatuated person very much
resembles that of a drug addict.*

When people say that relationships are serious, and that you shouldn't be quick to jump into love and romance, there is wisdom in that. Sometimes what looks like love is not. Sometimes it is infatuation. And infatuation can be like a very strong drug that just happens to be legal. Look back at the list of things that real love is. Real love is patient, trusting, caring, gentle, pure, not jealous. Compare those qualities to your relationships and see if they are lining up. If they're not, then chances are, it's not love.[3]

Test Yourself: Just a Crush or Something More?

1. **How often do you talk?**

    A. Never. I just stare non-creepily from a distance.
    B. Occasionally, in between classes and stuff.
    C. Several times a day.

2. **When you talk, it is usually . . .**

    A. We don't talk; I'm not sure the love of my life knows I'm alive.

B. Through text messages mostly.

C. In person or on the phone.

3. The first thought that pops into your mind when you see him or her is . . .

A. Wow! Looking good today!

B. I wonder if he/she really likes me.

C. What a kind and thoughtful person.

4. If your dream date has had a bad day, you . . .

A. Don't notice.

B. Wish he/she would quit complaining and pay more attention to you.

C. Listen, and then try to think of something cheerful to say or do.

5. How much do you know about him/her?

A. His/her class schedule and the best times to "accidentally" meet.

B. Who his/her friends are.

C. His/her thoughts about life, the future, God, and relationships.

6. The feature you find most attractive is . . .

A. Appearance.

B. The way he/she acts around you and your friends.

C. Personality, demeanor, looks, and intelligence.

7. **When you are together, you mostly talk about . . .**

A. My dream date doesn't know I exist, remember!?!
B. Yourself, or what's going on with people and school.
C. What's happening in your lives.

8. **You trust this person to . . .**

A. Be eye candy and that's about it.
B. Be a fun date.
C. Have your best interests and others' interests at heart.

9. **If your parents/close friends didn't like this person, you would . . .**

A. I haven't told my parents/close friends.
B. Ignore them. I make my own decisions.
C. Listen to them and talk it through with them.

10. **Your age is . . .**

A. 13 or younger.
B. Why does that matter?
C. Late teens. I know that's still young, but . . .

If you answered mostly As, then this is a crush. Pure and simple. And that's okay, it's natural. That's what teenage girls (and guys) do.

If you answered mostly Bs, you're thinking about yourself too much and what you can get out of a relationship. This isn't love or anything like it really, but it is a part of growing up. Just make sure you continue to grow *up* and *out* of this stage.

If you answered mostly Cs, you could be on your way to something deeper. Perhaps it's friendship; perhaps it's something more. You've broadened your horizons enough to start putting someone else before yourself. You're interested in more than just appearances and in what happens today. But be careful. Take it slow. And relax. Love is something that grows over time; it shouldn't be rushed. And remember, you're still a teen— a maturing, growing teen, but still a teen.

▶ It's NOT about You

These are the first words in a very famous book called *The Purpose Driven Life*.[4] I'll say them again, "It's not about you." These words are a great reminder that the things we experience, like love, aren't only about us. They are also about God. I understand that not everyone shares the same faith as me, so I'll try to explain. I know that Jesus was a historical figure who claimed to be *the* Messiah, which means "someone with a message." He didn't claim to be just any messiah; he claimed to be *the* Messiah, the person who came as the Son of God to love mankind and to sacrifice himself for it. I believe that Jesus was telling the truth. And because I believe that, I believe everything he said and taught. Many of his teachings have to do with love. In other words, because I am a Christian, my view of love doesn't just have to do with my opinion, it is shaped by Jesus, whose teachings I strive to pattern my life after. I'm not always great at this, if I can be the first to say it. But that is my goal even if I don't do it perfectly. You don't make every basket you shoot at, but you still try to make every shot you take. Kind of like that, but Jesus is the basketball. I'm not trying to preach at you, but I do want you to know that my faith shapes my view on subjects like love. And your views and faith and philosophies also do. It's impossible for them not to.

So, as a follower of Jesus, it's not just about me. In the book of Romans, it says, "Everything comes from God alone. Everything lives by his power, and everything is for his glory" (Romans 11:36 TLB). In other words, what we do with our lives, and the deep reason for love, is not just for ourselves. It is to connect with God, with all the things that he created, and with all the things he created in us. When I am standing on top of a mountain, looking out over the wilderness and at the clouds and the birds, it's hard for me to just think, *Oh, neato! These are great geographical features.* Instead, something in me makes me feel peace, connectedness, and pure humility. And when it comes to love, I can't but wonder why I need love—to give and receive it. It's not just about me anymore. I want to feel love, give love, and feel closer to God because of the love that I know he has for me. I know that it's about something more than myself.

I think love exists to bring us closer to God. That's me telling you what is really in my heart as I try to learn about love, just like you do. Don't worry; I don't think or see love becoming something less amazing because God is at the center of it. Just the opposite. I think that when we allow love to bring us closer to God, we, in return, experience love on a much deeper level than we could do on our own. I don't think letting God in will keep you from feeling all fuzzy and romantic and tickled over someone who makes your heart race. I think God will take those feelings to a deeper place of understanding. I believe love is not complete until it first rests in God. As Saint Augustine once said, "Because God made us for himself, our hearts are restless until they rest in him."

> *I believe love is not complete until*
> *it first rests in God.*

My tank of love is pretty small when I'm trying to keep it filled myself. I find that when it's filled with God's love, it runs better and it gives off a lot more love to everyone around me. It is our privilege and responsibility to learn how to love as God does, because God is love. It's not just about you. But it is about the One who thinks about you and loves all the time.

God really loves you. And so do I, but in a completely legal way. I checked with my lawyer, and I can say that.

6

JUST FRIENDS!?!

Who was the first American president? George Washington, right? You would be wrong. Peyton Randolph. Not only was he the first American president, but he was the first of fourteen people who were presidents before George Washington. It was Peyton Randolph who declared that the British were attacking America, and it was he who devised the Continental Army, placing George Washington as its commander-in-chief. Later, it was John Hancock who presided over the Declaration of Independence. It was not until April 30, 1789, that George Washington was sworn in as the president of the independent United States of America, but there were many "presidents" before ol' George.

You also might find it interesting to know that by the time George Washington was sworn in as president, he had only one real tooth left in his mouth. He had chronically terrible teeth, most likely due to the medicine that helped treat his malaria. He had false teeth made of hippopotamus and elephant ivory. That's right, the first president under the Constitution had a mouth full of hippo tusk. His dentures had a spring mechanism that made George have to forcibly keep his mouth shut, and it caused him a lot of pain. If you pick up a one-dollar bill, you will notice a portrait of the president with an apparent look of distress around his mouth, which is thought to have been deliberately portrayed by painter Gilbert Stuart.[1]

Some "common knowledge" really isn't that common—or it's incorrect. And some common words, like "friend," really shouldn't be as common as we treat them.

Chad,

Why am I the girl who guys want to be friends with, but nothing else? What's wrong with me? I don't know what makes me such a good friend, but unattractive in other ways! It's like the term "just friends" was made just for me. Help.

"just a friend," and hating it,

      —Sabrina

Hello Author Guy,

I try to be a pretty good guy. Girls always tell me that they really like me, but I don't ever seem to be able to find someone who likes me the way I want to like them. I see jerk guys who get all the attention from girls, and they treat the girls like crap. And the girl I like always comes to me to talk about everything, and I feel like I'm her boyfriend without her liking me the same way back. Why do girls do that? It seems to happen to me more and more. It's weird to talk about since we are guys, but I wondered what you had to say about it maybe.

      —Jake

There is a misconception about the term "just friends," and we'll get to that later. In fact, there are a lot of common misconceptions. Like the one about the first American president, for example. Some misconceptions are complex, and some are almost too basic to believe.

There are also a lot of misconceptions when it comes to people's relationships. And even more so with words like *love, romance, attraction, commitment,* and especially—*friends.* It seems that people often get confused by friendship—where to go with it, whether it is supposed to lead you somewhere else, or how to handle being friends. It's even more confusing when guy/girl relationships complicate themselves past the basic point of friendship.

I've been looking for a girl like you—not you, but a girl like you.

—Groucho Marx

➡ Wanna Be My Friend? Or Is That Too Awkward?

Friendship is a building block, my friend. But how do you even define being a friend? 'Cause to be honest with you, how can you really ever have a friendship if you have no idea what it is? So, as I usually like to do, let's start with a basic, common definition.

Friend: (noun)

1. *a person attached to another by feelings of affection or personal regard*
2. *a favored companion*
3. *an ally in a fight or cause; a supporter*
4. *a patron or supporter*[2]

Which all sounds good. A supporter, an ally, a person who has affection for you (not necessarily romantic), and someone who cares about your "'personal regard'" or well-being. That's a decent start to defining what a friend is.

Here are some of the funny—and kind of cheesy—definitions of friendship that float around in forwarded e-mails. *Oh my gosh, hurry! Send this to ten people in the next two minutes, or your pinky toe will fall off, and you won't find true love for thirty-one more years!* Yeah. Let me get right on that.

◎ If all my friends were to jump off a bridge, I wouldn't jump with them. I would be at the bottom to catch them. (Author's note: This is terrible advice. And why are you hanging around with people who jump off bridges? Is there water underneath? 'Cause that makes a big difference. One person falling on you hurts, let alone all of your friends. Just let one friend jump off the table onto you and see if you like it. You won't. Now imagine your friend falling on you from ten stories up. Visualize this scenario, and then never ever do it. Buy a bridge-jumper-catcher-thingy instead, and put it where they would land, for crying out loud.)

⊚ A true friend will see you through when others see that you are through.

⊚ A friend is someone who will bail you out of jail. A best friend is the one who will be sitting next to you in the cell, saying, "That was awesome." (Another author's note: I ran this by several police officers and judges, and they thoroughly disagreed with this friendship statement. Also, getting out of jail costs a lot of money and stays on your record.)

⊚ A friend to love with . . . a friend to play with . . . a friend to be with . . . a friend to stay with. (Awww, it rhymed.)

⊚ Friends are the bacon bits in the salad bowl of life. (Yet another author's note: Please don't call me bacon. People who have dealt with chubbiness don't appreciate it. *Cough, cough.* And I don't like salad, nor would I like to be something in a salad that someone else is eating. I take multivitamins, thank you very much.)

These quotes are a little cheesy—okay, these quotes are a *lot* cheesy. But they do describe some things about friendship. And that's a place to start. Especially before we get to the place where "just friends" doesn't feel good at all and is a struggle for the person hearing it.

What's the Point of Friendship?

Friendship is like a different kind of oxygen. People need friendship just as much as they need to breathe. We don't do well alone. We are built for life with others. We *need* to experience life with other people. We have to have care and affection in our lives. And that is what friends are for.

When babies aren't cared for, nurtured, or touched for long periods of time, really sad and strange things happen to them. In the first three years of life, the brains of infants who are neglected don't develop the same as in other infants. They have a hard time with motor skills, language, body language, stress levels in the body, and later the ability to identify feelings.[3]

We actually need people who are "just friends" as much, and even more, than we need romantic relationships. Though "just friends" is tough to hear when you're hoping for much more. But let's not let the term "just friends" minimize friendship. I promise you there is nothing minimal about real friendship. Everyone needs it. You need it, and without it, you are incomplete.

As iron sharpens iron, so one man sharpens another.
—Proverbs 27:17 NIV

Can You Really Be "Just Friends"?

That's a great question, and one that's been around a long time. I once heard a conversation that went something like this:

> LOGAN: Hey, let's do something sometime. Dinner and maybe a movie? . . . Just friends, I promise.
> ANNIE: Wait! Last week it was you who was saying that guys and girls can't be "just friends."

> LOGAN: Yeah, but I was talking about a lot of stuff. Are you sure I said that? When?
> ANNIE: Last Tuesday. You practically made a speech about it!

LOGAN: Wait! Hold on, I never said that exactly . . . I mean, yeah, that's right. Guys and girls can't be friends, but they can if they are dating someone else; then it works. This changes the earlier thing. But then that doesn't really work because then the boyfriend or girlfriend gets jealous when they want to know why you are such good friends with another guy or a girl. Why would you need the other person unless the person you are dating isn't good enough, right? And then, of course, you're like, "No, it's not like that. I really like you. They are just my friend. I'm not comparing them to you. I mean you are funny in a different way, sweetheart, that's all!" And then, of course, your boyfriend or girlfriend is just going to say you secretly love the other person and that saying you are just friends is a lie, which it probably is anyway. I guess I'm saying, I mean, are we joking? Of course, they can't be, unless maybe they were childhood friends, and they never really talk or know each other. And this brings me back to the earlier point, which is guys and girls can't be just friends.

In other words, it's super complicated. But let me simplify it for you. Can you ever really be "just friends" with the opposite sex? And my simple answer is . . . yes. And you'd better be able to, or you'll be in a world of hurt.

If you only view the opposite sex as potential for romantic relationships, then you are limiting the human experience. People are more than potential girlfriends and boyfriends. And if you only put on your romance goggles to view them, then a few things will happen:

⊚ You will only be looking at people to see what they can do for your needs.

⊚ You will miss out on people's unique identities, because you will limit them to their romantic capacity.

⊚ If you are a Christian, you will be ignoring the importance and wisdom of seeing one another as "brothers and sisters" in Christ, which opens up relationships well beyond just the romantic aspects.

⊚ You won't do as well in a job, or school, or anywhere else in life where you need to experience things with people of the opposite sex.

⊚ You will miss out on learning self-control and the experience of shaping your minds and hearts through your behavior. You don't have to be controlled by every thought and urge that pops up. It's what separates us from the mating habits of monkeys who can't control themselves and throw their own poo around, by the way.

Sure, there may come a time when you will develop feelings for a friend who just wants to be a friend. But some people believe that romantic feelings will always develop between friends. So unless they are interested in the other person romantically, they won't even try to have a friendship.

I have friends from high school, both guys and girls, whom I still know and love hearing from. I don't really sit on the phone and talk for hours with girls just for fun anymore; plus I don't have the time. But I can't imagine writing them out of my life just because I'm not interested in them romantically. What a limiting view.

I have a friend who just traveled around the country to raise money for an important charity. I can't wait to hear about that. When she started dating a guy very seriously, guess what? I couldn't wait to meet her boyfriend, because I was guessing that he was going to be a new friend. I want the best for my friends. When people put the *well-being* of their friends before their own desires, they are doing themselves and everyone else a noble thing.

The core of friendship is having other people's best interests in your mind and heart. With real friends, you forgo selfishness. If you just look at the opposite sex as potential dates, then you have really limited other people, as well as your own life. So let's stop putting limits on beautiful, God-given things, like people of the opposite sex.

➡️ The Friendship Zone: Should You Move out of It?

Hey,

There's a girl that I think is really awesome. She is a friend of mine, and there are times that I think maybe I like her more than that. A buddy of mine started talking to her, and I think he liked her, and then I really started wondering if I liked her, but I thought, *Why am I doing this only when he likes her? Is that right?* I think she likes me more than that, and so it is awkward. Sometimes when we are hanging out, I get the feeling that she wants us to be a couple. Thought you could help since you deal with this stuff. What do you think is the right thing to do?

—Lee

The question is specific, but the feelings aren't. Sometimes it's hard to know how *you* feel, and it's way more difficult to know how other people feel, if that is even possible.

The thing that I would recommend is not to be in a hurry. Feelings come and go, so don't go cheetah on your impulse feelings. If you are a real friend, then the friendship needs to be respected. Keep in mind that there are virtually no benefits to romantic relationships in high school versus good, deep friendships. There are very few upsides to going from friends to boyfriend/girlfriend, but there are a lot of downsides. My advice is to have fun, don't be controlled by your feelings, and allow time to be your guide. Good things don't happen in a panicked rush.

Hi, Awkward Creepster/Creepster-ette

Sometimes understanding "just friends" can get flipped around. And sometimes, to be honest, people can get just plain creepy. Just as in a romantic relationship, both parties have to agree to want to be friends. You can't force friendship any more than you can force love. And you don't have to accept friendship that is forced upon you.

Dear Chad,

I was wondering if you could help me with this problem I have.

There's this guy who is pretty much obsessed with me, but I really don't like him. He seemed nice at first, but I didn't like him like that and I said, "I don't have the same feelings for you. Can we just be friends?"

He said he understood, and yes, we could just be friends, but he still over-compliments (every single thing I say gets turned around into flattery) and flirts, and it's just crazy.

He would comment on every single status and a lot of my photos on Facebook until I blocked him from seeing my wall. The first thing he said when he next talked to me was, "Why can't I see your wall? Unblock me, this is about trust, and you don't trust or respect me. I'm being a nice guy, and I don't know what you're playing at." Then he posts a public status saying that sometimes he's too nice to people who don't deserve his trust or respect, and my friends all saw it. He turns it around and makes me look like the meanie.

It gets worse, because he thinks he's being a super nice guy and that he's being a good Christian by being "merciful" to me and still liking me even when I ignore him. When I tell him I don't like him, he says, "But God knows our hearts more than we know ourselves, and we can't know the future." When I tell him to stop liking me, he says that's like telling him to stop putting his faith in God, when God hasn't given him an answer yet. When I tell him I already gave him an answer, he says he's not worried, God has got his back. And when I tell him it's not all between him and God, that I have some say too, and it takes two to make a relationship, then he says, "I know it takes two, but I'm the one who's never going to give up."

Why would he say this? It's actually scaring me now, Chad. I told him that he was being obsessive, and he laughed at me and said, "I ain't obsessive." I told him he was scaring me and he said, "Aw, how cute."

I'm really angry and scared by how he's sort of forcing me to be his friend and almost trying to force me into a relationship through guilt and quoting verses and fear that he will post a horrible status about me. (He posts a lot of statuses about me.)

I hate how he's doing this to me. What do I do?

    —Stephanie

Hey, Stephalopolous, I'm *really* sorry about this. And yes, it's super annoying, and it's very unhealthy, and it's very immature, and it's just creepy. And it could even become dangerous. He is using God as a scapegoat for what he wants.

Both guys and girls can be guilty of doing these kinds of things. It happens all the time. When we want something—or someone—it can be easy to try and use anything to get it, even if that anything is God. Throughout history, God has often been the scapegoat for man's personal desires, greed, war, and a lot of other things that never resemble God or the character of Jesus Christ in any way. And I'm guessing that God doesn't like this, and he will have plenty to say about this face-to-face one day. Do you hear that, dudes of the Spanish Inquisition of 1478?

Love must be sincere. Cling to what is good. Be devoted to one another in brotherly love. Honor one another above yourselves.

—Romans 12:9–10 NIV

You are right in what you said and wrote. And you have the right to be angry and feel disrespected. God didn't make love or friendship one-sided. And he commands us to respect one another, not manipulate. And you should be able to tell this guy these things loudly and confidently, if necessary, and feel okay about it. Or call your big brother or other intimidating father fig-ure, and have him sit down with Mr. Manipulative and help him understand. I'd be glad to do it, but my editor says that it's not a good idea for many, many legal reasons.

When you are dealing with a bold and somewhat delusional individual, sometimes you have to bring this behavior out into the light so that others can see it and be there for you. This guy has just plowed through the "Let's Stop Here, Creepy" sign and is headed for some twisted territory. So tell your pastor, youth pas-tor, or your parents or his parents. And do it proudly. It says you simply aren't going to deal with what he's doing to you, and you don't mind telling other people it's not okay to disrespect you like that. You aren't tattling. You are sticking up for yourself. Don't let yourself become victimized by someone else's drama. Then set strong boundaries and stick to them. You could start with:

- "Leave me alone, period."

- "Don't talk to me again."

- "Get away from me."

- "You are disrespectful, and you are not going to manipulate me."

You know, stuff like that. Then ignore him completely, delete him from your Facebook account, and don't engage him in any way. Boundaries are good; keep making proper ones, and keep those boundaries strong. Oh yeah, and then stick by them.

P.S. Don't forget that God isn't the bad guy in these actions; the person is. God doesn't manipulate people like that. Don't let someone's creepy behavior be a distraction from the real God, who only has the best for you.

You are a sharp person; you will get through it. Be strong and keep your head held high. This can be a growing experience if you will allow it to be.

People deal with the "just friends" issue all the time. Sometimes you will be on the receiving end of the "I-just-want-to-be-friends" speech, and sometimes you will be the one saying it. It's not really natural for either party to just magically know how to do these things well. You aren't born knowing how to walk or drive a car. You have to learn. The same is true of that weird place between discerning feelings of friendship and feelings that go beyond it. It's a learning curve. So keep learning and be positive that other people will learn too. Just make sure you aren't making miniature dolls out of their hair or something. Yuck.

My Problem with "Just Friends"

My problem with the phrase "just friends" runs deep. As I said earlier, it makes friendship seem almost trivial. It makes it seem that romance is more important than "just being boring, stupid ol' friends" or that somehow friendship isn't enough. Do yourself and the other people around you a favor: take the "just" out of "just friends." Do you know what happens when you do that? You go from a question about not getting enough to a compliment of the highest regard.

Instead of asking, "Why do guys/girls want to be '*just* friends' with me?" Remove your head from your rear end and try asking, "Why do guys/girls want to be friends with me?"

Well, maybe because there is something incredibly likable about you, you weirdo. That's probably why. If someone said she wanted to be friends with me, I would take that as an amazing compliment. I like friends, and I like it when people like me back.

Try taking "just friends" as a compliment instead of a short-coming. You'll be surprised by how it can change your opinion of yourself. Why do people want to be friends with you? Probably because you have a lot to offer that isn't limited to going on a date.

Get out of the shallow end of relationships. Hop into the deeper waters. It's really nice and refreshing.

Bombing Your Friendships

How many people do you know who ruin perfectly good friendships? And how often is it because they "had to know" if it could be a romantic relationship or not? This happens a lot. Yes, you can have good, deep, and lasting friendships with the opposite sex. And no, it doesn't have to end with you falling in love or anything.

Sometimes people ruin friendships because they are lonely. Sometimes they confuse their feelings of admiration or closeness with intensely romantic love. Either way, here are a few things to consider on the subject.

I know a girl who is and has been a longtime friend of mine. But there was a time when that almost got messed up. I almost let our friendship be ruined by thinking that people who are close to one another and have close feelings have to act on those feelings, even the romantic ones. I always had a confusing feeling that lingered below the surface, as in "I wonder if she might have deeper feelings toward me." I had a hunch that she might feel this way. I mean, if you are a good friend and someone feels cared about and feels they can trust you, then sure, there is a chance that one person might perceive, or sometimes mistake, those traits for romantic feelings. People would occasionally say, "You two would be great together. Why aren't you dating?" but in my mind I always had the thought, *No, we wouldn't be good together. I don't have those feelings, but I love her as my friend in life.* And because we were good friends, we had a friendship that grew deeper. And of course I sometimes wondered about my feelings for her, and whether or not those feelings were supposed to lead to something more romantic. But I didn't want to lose my friendship. I realized that I was about to try to force something that wasn't there for me. It's weird, and it's hard to draw a distinct line where friendship crosses over into romance.

Fortunately, I didn't cross over that line, and I'm glad I didn't. It would have been bad for everyone. I would have hurt and confused my friend and probably ruined our friendship. Some people can realize they aren't romantically compatible and go back to being friends, but most people can't. Caring relationships with the opposite sex don't have to just be romantic. They can be deeply rooted in respect and care and support, and they don't have to be self-serving.

Are You Just Romancing Your Friendships?

There are several reasons why some people try to turn a friendship into a romance. Some of the most common ones are:

✓ Sometimes we do something called *projecting*. We project what we would like to see in other people. It's not fair to them, but it's also natural, and something we have to learn to keep in check. If you have done this, or do this, then what happens is that you often idealize the romantic feelings of someone you care about.

✓ Sometimes it's because the person is new and that's exciting. Sometimes those romantic feelings are because of who you hope that someone will be and not necessarily who he or she really is.

✓ Sometimes people have "neediness" that gets romanticized. In other words, you have needs that aren't being met, and you are looking for someone to come and help. This gets confusing with someone who is a friend, and suddenly it's more about them fulfilling *your* needs than a natural, mutual relationship that happens on solid footing.

✓ Loneliness is a big factor in why people try to turn friendships into something that they shouldn't be. Don't let loneliness be the engine that drives that car. It will wreck your car and you with it.

✓ Some people are in love with being in love. There's nothing wrong with loving romance; but if that becomes your life's focus, then you might find yourself trying to take friendships to a romantic level simply because you like romance so much.

✓ Some play the "mom" or "caregiver" role. Maybe you love babies and want to be a good mother or father. But that's not really a reason to take a trip down romance lane. This is a classic rescuer role; you want to help someone and care for them, and it's easy to romanticize those feelings. The person is there to help rescue or solve the problems of a friend. The friend then, in return, falls for the person who is caring about them. But in a lot of ways this is a parent/child relationship, and it eventually creates tension.

⅟. There is also the "Island Scenario." Sometimes it's proximity, or your physical closeness and geography to someone. If you are trapped for years on an island with someone of the opposite sex, there's a good chance that you'll eventually develop romantic and sexual feelings for that person. But much of that is simply because no one else is around.

People need to be balanced. They need a variety of places and people in their lives. You often find that people who might have been obsessed or crazy about someone in high school look back and laugh at themselves when they get to college. "What was I thinking? Why did I think I liked them that way?" And part of that is because we haven't expanded our experiences by meeting lots of people yet.[4]

Why Am I Always "Just Friends"?

This is really the question, isn't it? Or maybe it's actually not. Maybe there is a far deeper question. I mean, at the end of the day, doesn't the real question look more like one of these?

✓ Will someone like me?

✓ Will someone think that I am funny, that I am beautiful or good-looking?

✓ Will someone want to hold my hand, look into my eyes, and tell me that there is something special about me?

✔ Will someone ever want me to be his counterpart in life?

✔ Is there an amazing someone who will think I am amazing too?

These are the real questions we wonder about. It's not about friendship; it's about our longing to feel unique and loved and special to someone. And that doesn't have to do with boys and girls. It comes from somewhere different.

And now I'm going to hit you with a very, very heavy quote.

> The books or the music in which we thought the beauty was located will betray us if we trust to them; it was not in them, it only comes through them, and what came through them was longing. These things—the beauty, the memory of our own past— are good images of what we really desire; but if they are mistaken for the thing itself they turn into dumb idols, breaking the hearts of their worshipers. For they are not the thing itself; they are only the scent of a flower we have not found.
>
> —C. S. Lewis,
> The Weight of Glory

That is probably one of the deeper quotes I have ever come across, and it uncovers what's really going on with our hearts. We aren't longing for boyfriends or girlfriends. We are longing to be known, to be loved, and to feel significant. Every one of us. We spend our whole lives looking for those things. And so often we are disappointed because no one person can ever perfectly fulfill all of our longings.

In other words, it's not really about guys or girls or love or dating or friendships. These are the scent of the flower that we don't see. Our real search—whether we admit it or not—is for the Creator of those desires. God placed those burning desires within each of us—to be known, to feel loved, to be significant. And they can't ever be fulfilled by the things of this world that we mistakenly trust in, like prom dates or someone telling us we are hot. These things fall short. Every time. It's God—and only God—who perfectly fulfills those longings in us. He asks us to come and find our identity in him, to entrust our hearts to the One who created them in the first place.

> We aren't longing for boyfriends or girlfriends. We are longing to be known, to be loved, and to feel significant. And "just" being a friend is actually a pretty great place to start. There is no "just" in real friendship.

7

WHAT DO THEY WANT, ANYWAY?

Questions from Actual Students and Answers from Actual Me

Sometimes people want strange things. And sometimes what they want can backfire on them and be quite embarrassing. Take Napoleon, the emperor of France, for example. You know, like when people say someone who is small and acting all dominant has a Napoleon complex? Yeah, that guy. In 1807, Napoleon was so excited about a treaty that he created between several countries that he decided to celebrate by shooting a bunch of rabbits. I guess that was a pretty fun French celebration in the day. His chief of staff got him thousands of rabbits so that his staff could laugh and shoot Bugs Bunny and friends all afternoon.

Here's where the error occurred. His staff member ordered the wrong kind of thousands of rabbits, and they were tame instead of wild rabbits. So they liked people, and they were used to being fed by people. When the herd of rabbits was released, they spotted a tiny little man in a big hat—Napoleon—and mistook him for the feeder. So the hungry rabbits sprinted toward Napoleon at about 35 mph. The mighty emperor was chased down by thousands of hungry, aggressive, large rabbits, and he had to flee while beating them off with his bare hands in front of a large crowd. They tore off most of his clothing and bit him all over his body. He finally had to speed away in his coach, beat up and covered in shame from the bunny beat down.[1]

109

Be careful what you wish for; I guess you might get it in a weird way. This next bit should be much less painful than being attacked by thousands of angry rabbits, but here goes. You've got questions; I've got answers. Sometimes the truth will sting, but we have a lot to talk about.

The mystery of understanding what men and women want is also the answer, and we must spend our whole life learning that answer.

—Chad

What Do Guys Want, Anyway!?!

Hey,

I'm sure you get this all the time, but I'm just going to say it anyway. Is there something that guys want? I mean, seriously! What do guys want? You have to know the answer to this. I have so many questions about the guys in my life and my experiences with guys, but I guess at the bottom of it is that I don't know what they want. Does anyone know? Maybe you do, but don't worry; I won't be disappointed if you don't.

—Hanna

That's a fair question that Hanna asks. And it's a big one. And big questions don't have simple answers. Well, they do and they don't. There is no way to answer for what all guys want, especially when some don't know themselves. And lots of guys want lots of different things. But there are some things that all guys have in common and want desperately. And, as it turns out, there are some questions about guys that just about all girls have. So here are my best answers to some of the most common things girls really want to understand about those creatures who can smell so awful but then can be so good, so funny, so kind, or so cruel.

Q: Do teenage guys want something that is fundamentally different from teenage girls?

A: To be blunt, yes. There is a strange disconnect between the genders when it comes to puberty, and the physical, mental, and emotional state of guys as compared to girls. I mean for some guys and girls it might be the same, but for most, it is completely different.

Girls tend to care more deeply about relationships at younger ages than guys do. It's no one's fault; part of it is biological, and part of it is social. The answer to this situation is one that most people hate: time. Most teenage guys are simply not as emotionally consumed by the desire to have deep relationships, because there is something in their subconscious that lets them know that they are not ready for that yet. They're not ready to be married or to be dads while they're still trying to figure out their own personalities and what they want to do after high school. And that's what deep relationships are headed for.

There are always exceptions. Some girls don't care about relationships, and some guys are relationship hounds. But for the most part, yes, there is a fundamental difference. That's why being a teenager is not meant to teach you how to be in deep romantic relationships. Being a teenager is about preparing for adulthood and having fun and learning the social dynamics that you will need in the future, which will eventually lead to that smoochy-smoochy you think about so much.

> Life was so much easier when your clothes didn't match and boys had cooties!
>
> —Unknown

Q: Why do guys say they really like you, but then they just want to be friends?

A: Well, probably because they are confused, just like you get confused, or are confused by them. Maybe they do have certain feelings of interest toward you, but they don't know what that means. They shouldn't really be telling you they like you because it's confusing, but I doubt they really know what to do with those confusing feelings. Probably a lot like you. If someone is confused about how he or she feels about you, then it's good to stick to friendship. Because you don't want to feel like someone likes you one day and then pushes you aside the next. That sounds like about as much fun as being hit by a car. So maybe don't do that. My friend got hit by a car. He said it was not great.

Q: Why are guys so "hot" and then so "cold"?

A: Again, guys don't have themselves figured out yet, just like you don't have yourself figured out. Sometimes your mood changes, and sometimes a guy's mood or "mode" changes. Guys are trying to deal with hormone changes, the stress of school and/or family, and other internal struggles that you may not know about. My suggestion is that you don't take everything personally because there is a chance that it doesn't have to do with you. Just like your mood swings don't have to do with only one thing. If you want us guys to cut you some slack, then return the favor. *But* if a guy is being mean and harsh in a way that friends just don't do, and it happens all the time, just wave bye-bye. It's not worth wasting your time.

Q: How do you know if a guy really likes you?

A: Congratulations, you have now asked the most asked question of the last two years. How do you know if a guy likes you? Well, sometimes it's obvious. He will put himself in your presence a lot more often. He might go out of his way to talk to you, to talk to your friends, or to let you know through other people that he thinks nice things about you. In that case, it isn't so hard to figure out that he likes you. The confusion comes when a guy sends mixed messages, acting interested one second and completely unconcerned the next. If that's the case, then you might not know whether or not he really likes you, and you should protect yourself.

In the bigger picture, though, this is not so much about girls. This is a guy issue. Girls want a guy who is kind, but confident. There is a simple rule that I have when it comes to this. At some point, if a guy likes you, he needs to be able to look you in the eye and let you know that he really likes you, and then he needs to back that up with his actions. If he can't do this, he's not building up the confidence muscles he's going to need in life, and that will affect both you and him. You can't build up a guy's muscles or courage for him. All you can do is provide an appropriate time and place for him to take the dive. Guys need to be able to do this, and you are worth it.

At some point, if a guy likes you, he needs to be able to look you in the eye and let you know that he really likes you, and then he needs to back that up with his actions.

Q: Why can guys be so mean?

A: I think guys can be mean for the same reasons that girls can be mean. We are human, and we are full of fault. If you eat bad food, you become unhealthy. You won't live as long, you'll get fat, and you will sweat too much. In much the same way, if you live poorly, you'll probably be angry, hurt, and alone. And all that will come out in weird ways and on other people.

Sometimes guys have a lot of aggression that they don't know how to deal with, and it comes out as anger. Maybe it's something in their family; maybe it's how they are feeling inside. This isn't an excuse, just an explanation. You should also know being mean or angry is always a cover-up feeling. That means that the guy is using anger to cover up the fact that he is hurting inside. People who are feeling great and are healthy don't go around being cruel. There's just no reason to be. Having said that, it's not your job to fix that inside hurt for him.

Sometimes guys feel the need to compete. As a girl, you probably don't see the underlying rules and structures that exist in the world of guys. You don't know the pressure they feel to assimilate, or blend in. But it's just as real as the social world of girls. A world that most guys totally don't understand. Just so you know.

So you can try to understand why guys are being mean and gain some perspective. But you might also need to simply avoid people who cause pain in your life. Jumping in front of a train to stop it probably won't work. And it will hurt a whole lot. So pray for them instead. It helps. Promise.

Q: Why does it seem like so many guys are obsessed with sex? Is that really what they want? Do they want anything else?

A: There are some guys who really do get obsessed with girls and bodies and sex. It's what they think they want, and oftentimes they pursue it like a weird, out-of-control dog in heat. Unfortunately, they won't ever catch what it is they are chasing, and it will leave them unsatisfied.

There are certain biological parts of this that can't be ignored. And it's not just guys who have sexual desires; they are just more blunt about it. Well, actually there are plenty of girls who are blunt about it too. Girls have many of the same physical desires. The problem is that the body is built for sex before the heart can handle it—for both guys and girls. Yeah, guys have urges, but it doesn't mean we have to be controlled by them. Just because I'm mad and want to punch someone doesn't mean that I can't stop myself. But it's the habits we practice every day that build the patterns in our minds and hearts.

So to answer this question, in my heart I want to say no. Sex is not the thing that guys really want. I know it looks like it, but it's not just sex: it's what sex is supposed to provide. Love, pleasure, satisfaction. And we know the teens who do have sex don't feel this. So there you go. Some guys are obsessed with it, and unfortunately, they are running after a mirage in the desert, and they won't be satisfied with what they find. Sex is not just sex. It takes a person, and a person has a heart, and there's a lot within those hearts.

Not all guys are that way, though. And I meet them all the time. I'm proud to say I know many, and I'm glad to call them friends. Besides, you don't have to concern yourself with the entire world of guys, just the guy who will be the right fit for you. It's a lot less overwhelming than thinking of three and a half billion boys at once. That's too much cheap body spray cologne to handle anyway.

Q: Why do guys get so easily offended? Or do they?

A: Yes, they do . . . sometimes. Guys are sensitive; they simply show it in different ways than girls. They are more likely to bottle up and internalize feelings before they share them with people—if they share them at all. It's not true that guys have no feelings and girls just have lots of them. Most research shows that girls and guys experience the same amount of feelings. We just experience them differently and express them *very* differently.

So in the same way that you hope people are kind

to you and don't hurt your feelings, it kind of goes without saying that you should be considerate of guys too. Just because you may not see all their feelings, it doesn't mean they can't experience pain. The golden rule exists for a reason.

Q: Do guys ever mature?

A: I hope so. But seriously, yes, most of them do. The thing you need to remember is that it's a choice they have to make, and it's the habits they choose that matter the most. I know some guys who were absolute tool-bag, crazy-mean, lost punks who turned out to be incredible men later on. I also know some men who started out great and have now regressed and act like seventh graders. It's a personal decision, and the friends they choose will influence that a lot.

Oh, and you have to grow up, too, or your question doesn't count.

Q: Why do guys try to text nasty or sexual things?

A: For a few reasons. But before that, this goes both ways—plenty of girls do it too. First, no one is telling them or showing them that they can't. Or they aren't doing it sternly enough, meaning letting a parent or teacher or, if necessary, the police know. If a guy is texting you this stuff, it's up to you to set the boundaries in your life and to get help when you need it.

Second, it's easier for guys to text things than to say them. Texting still gets their adrenaline going and is physically exciting and addicting, but it's "safer" than trying it in person. It's easier. Easy things are cheap though, and girls don't deserve to be cheapened. The way to a girl's heart just isn't in some text message that takes ten seconds of dirty thoughts.

Third, guys fish. So do girls. People try to throw some bait out there and see who is willing to take it. It's a cheap way to catch something, but people do it. And one of the reasons that guys and girls do this is because other people take the bait. Again, it cheapens all that is good about romance and love. I hope you won't do that or let it be done to you.

Also, if you and a guy are sending and receiving sexual pictures, you should know that that's illegal because you're minors. You could get into serious trouble. Serious. The Internet can be a nasty place where people get their pictures placed. And they don't go away. Ever. You don't have to experience this to figure it out.

Q: When do guys figure out what they want, anyway? Or do they ever?

A: They'll probably figure it out when you do. Oh, and then when you figure out what you want, it will probably change, because people change and lives change.

So when do guys figure out what they want? Well, I'm still figuring it out. I started viewing relationships a lot differently when I was about twenty-five or twenty-six, though that may change as I grow older. And I'm still figuring out what I want to do with my career and where it will take me. I think this is normal. Some people take more time, other people less. Some never figure it out. But if I'm just giving numbers to you, I'd say the midtwenties are a good starting point. It's when the frontal lobe of your brain develops, which gives you forward thinking. It's also the time when you map out your life a little more clearly and start down the path that will truly define it. If you are fifteen, sorry, you have to wait ten years. But don't just waste your time waiting. This is your life—keep trying to figure it out, no matter what age you are.

▶ What Do Girls Want, Anyway!?!

Chad,

I have a lot of questions about girls. I'm a pretty normal guy, and I don't try to be like any of the stereotypes of guys. I just try to be myself. But I listened to you talk to us, and there are a lot of things that are really different between girls and us guys. I know I can't understand it all or anything, but I guess it's hard to know what girls want. They always seem confused about what they want, so how am I supposed to know? I mean if I don't know what I want, how can someone else know? Just seems weird. Thought I would ask what you have to say about the subject. Thanks.

—Conner

The same is true for the prettier gender. Although guys may not be as vocal about declaring their confusion about girls as girls are about them, they still have lots of questions. They want to know about the gender that has better handwriting, higher voices, creative clothing, colorful earrings, smiles that drive them nuts, and all kinds of their own confusing behaviors. Sorry, if it's true of guys, then it's also true of you girls. We're all in the same boat. Keep rowing; it's the only option we have.

Q: Why are girls so emotional? Why don't they seem to be able to understand and control their emotions?

A: Mostly because they *have* emotions. So sue them. Guys are emotional too; we just usually aren't as in touch with those emotions, or as able to describe them. By age seven, females know twice as many words to describe their feelings as boys do. There is nothing wrong with being emotional. At the same time, I understand that it's confusing when a girl doesn't seem to be able to control her emotions. Part of this may be that she just needs to learn to do better. That's why there is a whole chapter in this book devoted to crazy, mixed-up feelings.

Another part of girls' emotional makeup has to do with the chemistry of their bodies. A guy will never understand the hormonal changes that girls in puberty experience, how their brains change, the overwhelming feelings of comparison, and the uncertainty of their own beauty and value. On top of that, they have menstrual cycles and huge mood swings that are hard to control. They go from feeling fun and pretty one day to lousy, ugly, and bloated the next. So try to give them a break. Don't try to understand it all, because you never will. Just accept and do your best to be kind and courteous. And make sure you don't take it all personally. Odds are it doesn't have much to do with you. Thicken your skin a little bit.

> Girls are like cell phones. They like to be talked to, but push the wrong button, and you'll be disconnected.
>
> —Unknown

Q: How do you know if a girl likes you?

A: This is where you need to learn to be smart. You aren't born with the ability to read books, and you aren't born with the ability to read girls. You have to learn. It's a cat-and-mouse game, whether you like it or not, except there's a chance that the mouse wants to be caught.

If a girl likes you, she might tell you. Girls do that a lot more these days. But even if she does just come out and say it—while you as a guy you might be flattered—you'll also notice that it's not as satisfying as having to figure it out with some effort and take some action on your own behalf. We as guys like to earn things, and that includes the attention or affection of girls.

Having said that, here are a couple of clues: If a girl is interested in you, she will probably try to be around you more. If she is smart, she will present opportunities for you to approach her and talk to her. It's said that guys first fall in love with their eyes and girls with their ears. So if a girl is interested in you, that means she wants to get to know you, and she wants you to get to know her. You need to be gentle but assertive if you like her back. Talk with her in a personal way, asking questions about her and finding ways to let her know about you. If you have some common interests or places that you go, then ask her if she'd like to do something with you sometime. Girls like to be asked out; it makes them feel special. So do your best, be confident, and be a gentleman. The right girls like that. I'm 99.9 percent sure. I think.

We're all in the same boat. Keep rowing; it's the only option we have.

Q: Do girls want sex or the sexual stuff as much as guys do? You only hear that guys are creeps for wanting that stuff.

A: A very fair question. A girl just wrote me asking me if I would talk about how both guys and girls struggle with things like pornography. She felt as if people only say that lust and porn are issues that guys deal with, when in fact guys and girls both struggle with them, just in slightly different ways. Girls have sexual desires too, and they shouldn't feel awful for it, just like guys shouldn't. I do think it's unfair that we mostly talk about guys. Perhaps it's just because guys are generally a lot more open, outgoing, and joking about the sex stuff, and girls tend to keep it inside. This makes girls more likely to feel ashamed of those feelings or that there is something wrong with them.

The main difference is that girls and guys associate sex with different things, and they experience sex differently. It's very difficult, if not impossible, for a girl to *not* associate sex with being cared about and loved. So although she may have those sexual desires, she is less likely to do those things with a stranger or in a way that has no meaning for her. Some girls do, but trust me, if you heard their stories, you wouldn't think it was a good choice. Sex is a form of love. Without the love, it becomes something entirely different.

Both guys and girls do have sexual desires, but neither of you have to be controlled by them.

Q: What are girls attracted to in a guy? Is it the physical stuff, or is it something else? It's confusing.

A: Yes and definitely yes. It's a mixture of things. And it's probably a little different from what guys are attracted to in a girl, at least initially, in my opinion. Girls today are more focused on the physical appeal of guys than they were even five years ago, and a whole lot more than they were twenty years ago. After all, they are being sold all the same pictures and commercials of perfectly ripped guys, asking them to fixate on the physical aspects first. And of course this affects them. It's the same way that guys get sold pictures of hot girls wearing hardly any clothing.

But there is a lot more than just the physical. Girls seem to have an ability to see the whole person a little more than guys. Again, that's just my opinion. Girls just aren't as fixated on looks. They are usually attracted to confidence. (Not to be confused with cockiness.) They also tend to be attracted to guys who can make them laugh and those who have good eye contact without staring, as well as certain smells, certain heights, and certain voices. After this, it really becomes an individual preference. Girls are a mystery, and sometimes what they like is too.

The best thing you can do is avoid being a chameleon. The more you are simply you, the more someone will appreciate that. You only need that one special girl. Any more than that will cause you serious problems.

Q: Why do so many girls wear makeup and try so hard to look good or "natural"? Doesn't that defeat the purpose?

A: This is another one of those things that guys probably don't understand. I have never woken up and
thought, *I want to feel beautiful today.* I would probably punch myself if I had that thought. But I'm a
guy. I do know that. Girls need—among other
things—to feel valued, pretty, confident, and
beautiful.

   I know what guys mean about girls trying so hard
with their looks, clothes, and makeup. It bothers me
too. But guys overcompensate at the gym, with macho
attitudes, and lots of other stuff too. I wish that girls
would find balance. But I also know that girls like to
get dressed up and feel special and look good. Just
accept it.

   Most girls will wear some level of makeup, and
anything you say to change it or suggest that they
shouldn't will only get you a bad result. Trust me. The
best thing that you can do is let them know that you
like them just the way they are and focus on the inner
qualities that you appreciate and value.

*Girls need—among other things—to feel valued,
pretty, confident, and beautiful.*

Q: Why do so many girls have such a hard time getting
along with other girls?

A: That's a great question. Just like the social dynamic
of guys can be exclusive, the social dynamics of girls

can be equally, if not more, exclusive and even treacherous.

It's been said that if a guy wants to feel better than another guy, he will outcompete him. Run harder, swim faster, be funnier, make more money, whatever. And sometimes a girl, in order to feel superior to another girl, will simply cut the other girl down to make herself taller.

Also, once puberty happens, girls' hormones and bodies change earlier and faster than guys. It's the first time in their lives that they physically compare themselves to the outward appearance of other girls. In other words, there is a competition for beauty, whether or not they like it, and they find themselves feeling stuck in that competition without much of a choice. That competition can be overwhelming and make getting along with other girls more difficult.

Q: How do I know if a girl is flirting with me?

A: Body language, my friend. There is a whole chapter in *Guys Are Waffles, Girls Are Spaghetti* about it. If a girl is flirting, she will make more frequent eye contact. She will stand with better posture, putting her shoulders a little farther back. She will laugh more often at what you say to let you know that you are funny. She will smile much more often, and when she talks, her voice might be slightly higher. This is attractive to a guy. Don't ask me why; just trust me.

She will also do things like fiddle with her hair. This is because it releases hormones called *phero-mones*, and without going into detail, they help build attraction in the same way a nice perfume does.

She probably won't be aware that she is doing all of these things, but it's your job to pay attention. As I often say, your body always talks before your mouth does.

Q: Why do girls go to the bathroom in groups or pairs?

A: I don't know firsthand, and I'm proud to say that. Possibly for support, probably to talk. Maybe to talk about you, maybe about kangaroos. It's just that way. Accept it. You'll never stand on the surface of the sun, and you'll never be able to comprehend certain facts about the universe. One of those facts is why girls use the restroom as a social experience.

Q: How do you know ahead of time how a girl is going to be in a relationship? Like how she will be as a girlfriend or as a wife?

A: I think that's complex. People are unpredictable, but you can try to understand certain things. People have patterns. The more you get to know a girl, the more you will see patterns in her life, good or bad. And the closer you become to her, the more you can ask about those patterns in a loving way.

Family is a good place to look, although people shouldn't be defined wholly by their families. Some-times great people get stuck with lousy families. But if a girl has a strong, close family, then certain things about relationships will be easier for her.

You can also take tests. There are a lot of great resources out there that help people understand themselves and each other. There are the Myers–Briggs Test, DISC Tests, and Discover Your Strengths tests, along with thousands more for individuals and couples to help them learn more about their personalities, what they want to do, and how they see relationships.[2]

Of course, openness and honesty are always part of great relationships. And if you pray, then pray. Surround yourself with wise people who have experience and are willing to guide you. Your eyes are only one set, and other people's vision can help make things clear. Give it time, keep your eyes open, and keep learning along the way.

Q: Do girls want more than guys are capable of giving as teens?

A: Again, that depends on the girl—and the guy. Simply put, if a girl is healthy, balanced, taking care of herself, and focusing on her future as well as the present, then no.

If she is not healthy, not finding balance, or has hurts she is trying to fix with another person, then probably. Some needs can't be met by a guy. For example, if it's love from her father that she's missing, a guy won't be able to fill that void.

But plenty of girls out there are willing to give and get in normal, healthy, fun ways. The only thing that you need to give—or ask for in return—is friendship and care. Anything else will tilt the balance and cause stress. You don't need any more stress as a teenager. Life is tough enough.

▶ Look for Maps

This in no way answers all the questions that you have about the opposite sex. They can't be answered in one book, or even a whole library. And one set of answers won't work for everyone. The world is big, and the heart is complicated.

My best suggestion is to find a map, a guide, a leader to help you wander through life's questions and relationship struggles. Friends help, and good parents are an amazing help. But for me I have always found that God has left his imprints all over the world, and all over the hearts of other people. The principles in the Bible are just as true today as they were when they were written. They are the principles of honesty, kindness, consideration, adventure, friendship, truth, love, purpose, joy, suffering, valuing yourself, working hard, encouraging others, and—perhaps most important—knowing that we are already loved. I have found when I get distracted from these core principles, I start to wonder about all the small questions. But when I focus on God's principles, many of my questions are answered for me. I cannot explain it. I will just say that it is a truth in my life, even when times are hard. I believe God will do the same for you.

So what do guys and girls want, anyway? Ultimately, the same thing—to live, to love, and to be loved in return. And that's something that will never change.

8

CRAZY, DUMB, AND MIXED-UP FEELINGS

Did you know that elephants are afraid of mice? How weird is that, right?

If anything doesn't make sense, it's the thought of a four-ton beast that can smash a car by stepping on it, running from a six-ounce, squeaky mouse that's just looking for some cheese.

But a lot of things don't make sense in life—and not just in the animal kingdom. There are things that are just completely confusing too. I myself like animals. I've even thought about owning a pygmy elephant one day, but I think I'll just stick to my dream of a monkey that rides around on a miniature horse in the backyard instead. It seems like there is too much poop involved with elephants—no matter how pygmy-sized they are. If you've witnessed this, then you know, and I'm sorry.

All Mixed-Up Inside ◀

I was feeling stressed-out and overwhelmed not long ago. I felt lonely and just wanted to get away. So I went snowboarding by myself, thinking it would help. And guess what? No. I sat on the top of a mountain, thirteen thousand feet up, looking out over trees and mountains, and I realized that what I thought I was feeling wasn't accurate. Then I walked around town by myself and ate alone. These are things that can sometimes make me happy, but I wasn't enjoying myself. I just felt worse. I was wrong about my feelings, and I was wrong about the solution to them. I was in a beautiful place, looking at beautiful things all by myself. Sometimes it's helpful for me to be alone, but sometimes I listen to my dumb, mixed-up feelings when they are wrong. Feelings are major factors in our lives. They don't only affect us, but they can affect all of our relationships and how we handle our relationships. And you know what? Feelings can be misleading. A lot, actually.

I'd like to share a letter I received not long ago.

Chad,

I feel like I am in a fight with my own mind, and I think I'm going to lose. I have always struggled with hating myself. I didn't think I had any value whatsoever. I've never had many friends, and for some reason, I've always worried what people thought of me. I feel like I am tortured inside and I have no control over the things that come into my mind and the feelings that flood my life. And I'm too scared to get to know someone for fear they won't like me. I've struggled with thoughts of suicide. I have hated myself and all these feelings for a long time, and I think about ending my life.

—Lindz

First, if you're feeling as bad as Lindz, find someone you trust to talk to. Now. Seriously. Put down the book and go. You're still here? Go now.

Some people make the mistake of living only by their

feelings. Others make the mistake of never knowing or listening to their feelings enough. But I'll tell you this: Feelings are critical. They can be lifesaving or life-taking factors in your life, and you have to learn to deal with them. Your school, your friends, your job, your future husband or wife, your children, and every single other important thing that you will ever have in your life will be affected by your feelings. And what you do with your feelings will affect every part of your life, in the most important ways. Do *not* underestimate feelings or shy away from understanding why they are there and what's underneath them.

Feelings can be misleading.
A lot, actually.

Your emotions are connected to both your brain and your heart. The two are inseparable. As a teenager, you should know that the emotional center of your brain is on overload, and it can drive you crazy at times. It's not your fault. It's just what happens when your brain and body create insane new chemicals and testosterone and estrogen in amazing levels. The part of your brain that has to do with higher functioning and reasoning is the frontal lobe, and it's still developing. So your ability to think through your emotions and cope with them is also still developing. And this not-yet-fully-developed part of your brain is demonstrated in all kinds of teen behavior.[1] Such as:

driving recklessly

being controlled and overwhelmed by your feelings

obsessing about current and previous relationships

becoming clingy and overcommitted

surrounding yourself with constant social drama and living in anxiety over superficial issues

opposing teachers and authority figures with aggression instead of reason and persuasion

 choosing people based solely on aesthetic appeals, such as popularity, physical appearance, social dominance, or sexual desire

 lacking emotional self-control

being sexually promiscuous

 not understanding or practicing boundaries (Boundaries are commonly mistaken as rules to keep you from doing things. They're not. FYI.)

 texting, sexting, and putting yourself in compromising physical, verbal, and emotional situations[2]

Just because this part of your brain may not be fully developed, it doesn't mean that you can't learn to choose to control some of these feelings and actions. It's difficult, but completely possible. If you have ever been attacked or flooded by your feelings (and I know I have been), it can be hard to know why those feelings are there. And it can be especially hard to know what to do about them. We aren't born with the tools to just fix our feelings. We have to learn.

One important thing to learn is to identify your feelings. If you cannot identify your feelings, then you cannot soothe yourself or be soothed by someone else. In other words, you've got to know what you are feeling before you can do anything about it. One of the most prominent psychologists can observe a married couple for less than two minutes and predict with 80 to 94 percent accuracy whether or not they will stay married. He's done it accurately for almost twenty years.[3] **Here's the secret: The key to whether or not a relationship will last—and you need to know this—is how well you can calm *your own* overwhelming feelings.** Another key has to do with how well another person can help you soothe your feelings, but even that isn't as much about the other person as it is about you. If you can't identify your feelings and soothe them, then you will probably experience what is called *emotional flooding*.

When you become emotionally flooded, you may panic, run away, yell, scream, or even hurt other people. Your body goes nuts. You may experience a rapid heart rate, elevated blood pressure (which older people care about more than you), muscle convulsions, dehydration, adrenaline rushes, or rapid breathing. You may have some or all of these symptoms. Either way, you are no longer in control of what you are feeling; instead, you are being controlled by your feelings. And that is a scary place to be, because it means you are out of control. And bad things can happen when you become out of control.

Life Happens

Sometimes things happen in life with hardly any warning, if any at all. For example: Amy is sitting in math class. She gets a text from her friend that says the guy she likes, and who she thought liked her back, took Tara out last night and they made out. He had just told Amy a few nights before that he likes *her* a lot and loves being around her. Amy's heart starts to pound, she feels sick, and she starts to hyperventilate. Her throat tightens up, and she is confused. She holds back tears of hurt, and yet she feels angry and enraged—all at the same time. She wants to scream and hit something, but she also wants to cry. She is emotionally flooded. This wasn't a situation she chose to be in, but life and the tough stuff in it have sent a river of emotion in her direction. And it was one she probably never saw coming.

Feelings Happen

Sometimes feelings just happen. You can't keep them from popping up all the time—and you shouldn't. Feelings don't happen from nothing, but they actually happen in what is known as the *limbic system* of the brain. Sorry to go all scientific on you. The limbic system is an area that we have less control over than some other areas of the brain. In other words, feelings can pop up without your choosing, just like your hand reacts if it touches a hot stovetop.

When people are emotionally flooded, they can make the worst decisions, and oftentimes the most destructive ones, for themselves and for other people. Although you can't control the emotional flood, you can control what you do when the flood happens.

What's That You Didn't Say?

About 80 to 90 percent of how we express our feelings doesn't have to do with the use of words. It's called *nonverbal behavior*. Basically, we communicate a lot without the use of our mouths. If we don't identify our feelings and try to deal with them, they will find other—nonverbal—ways to come out in our lives. For example:

Your facial expressions may betray your inner thoughts and feelings.

 Your patience with other people may be limited and your temper short.

 Your feelings overwhelm you and distract you from the present moment and the people in it.

Feelings are part of your life. Accept it. Learn to identify them and figure out ways to deal with them. Your feelings can be your worst enemy, or they can actually become a trusted friend and guide. They can help guide you instead of leaving you stranded in the woods with no map. To help you make friends with your feelings, I've included a few pointers at the end of the chapter.

Your feelings can be your worst enemy, or they can actually become a trusted friend and guide.

Feelings: What to Do with Them Since You Can't Get Rid of Them

I'm Feeling . . . Ummm . . .

Some people can identify only a few basic feelings; others many more. I'm not going to scream in your ear, but I can tell you that the more of your feelings you can identify, the better. But let's start with the basics. Here are some more descriptive words for feelings that fall into the "basic" feeling categories.

Categories of Feelings

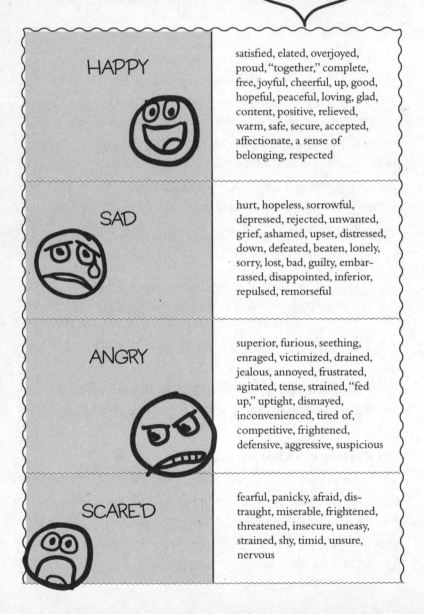

HAPPY	satisfied, elated, overjoyed, proud, "together," complete, free, joyful, cheerful, up, good, hopeful, peaceful, loving, glad, content, positive, relieved, warm, safe, secure, accepted, affectionate, a sense of belonging, respected
SAD	hurt, hopeless, sorrowful, depressed, rejected, unwanted, grief, ashamed, upset, distressed, down, defeated, beaten, lonely, sorry, lost, bad, guilty, embarrassed, disappointed, inferior, repulsed, remorseful
ANGRY	superior, furious, seething, enraged, victimized, drained, jealous, annoyed, frustrated, agitated, tense, strained, "fed up," uptight, dismayed, inconvenienced, tired of, competitive, frightened, defensive, aggressive, suspicious
SCARED	fearful, panicky, afraid, distraught, miserable, frightened, threatened, insecure, uneasy, strained, shy, timid, unsure, nervous

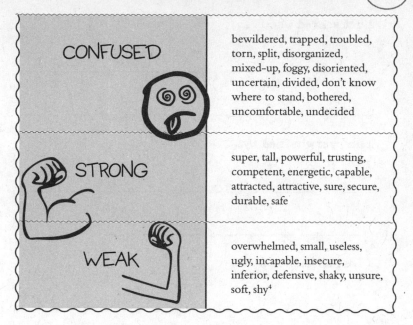

CONFUSED	bewildered, trapped, troubled, torn, split, disorganized, mixed-up, foggy, disoriented, uncertain, divided, don't know where to stand, bothered, uncomfortable, undecided
STRONG	super, tall, powerful, trusting, competent, energetic, capable, attracted, attractive, sure, secure, durable, safe
WEAK	overwhelmed, small, useless, ugly, incapable, insecure, inferior, defensive, shaky, unsure, soft, shy[4]

I know this next part may seem elementary, but it might help you identify some of your feelings with a little more depth. If you want. I myself have done this sort of thing a lot before, and I can say that writing things down makes more of a difference than you might think. Try answering these questions.

I become angry when . . .

_____

_____

I am lonely when . . .

_____

_____

I get scared when . . .

_____

_____

I am overwhelmed by . . .

_____

_____

I feel shame when . . .

_____

_____

I am hurt when . . .

_____

_____

I am confused when . . .

_____

_____

I am happy when . . .

_____

I feel strong when . . .

Easy as 1, 2, 3

Learning how to deal with your feelings—and thus avoiding being miserable—is not easy, and it takes a while. But you will either control your feelings, or you will be controlled by them. The easiest way to deal with your feelings is to follow these three steps.

1. Pray.

Calm yourself, slow down your breathing, and fix your thoughts on God. It will help, and he will help. Quiet prayer can provide peace and give you a break from being flooded by feelings.

2. Identify.

Try to identify the feelings *behind* the overwhelming ones. If you are angry, the odds are that you are really feeling a lot more than just anger, like maybe confusion, hurt, or being victimized, used, or devalued. If you can identify and deal with those feelings, the overwhelming feelings may take care of themselves.

3. Talk.

I know, I know. You've heard it before, but go talk to someone. We aren't meant to be alone. But be careful! Finding the right or wrong someone to confide in can make all the difference. Try to find someone who is a good listener, who doesn't try to give hasty or irrational advice, and who validates how you are feeling, while also giving you another perspective on the situation. He or she should be someone you trust to have your best interests in mind. Someone who won't share your secrets with anyone who will listen. And make sure their wisdom comes from a source that is also wise—like the Bible.

Drs. John and Linda Friel once wrote that the best way to deal with feelings is to follow this sequence:

FEEL ➤➤ **THINK (maybe for a while)** ➤➤ **Then ACT**
Then repeat the process.[5]

Feelings are powerful, and they are part of life. Learning to experience feelings, to identify and understand them, to learn what is causing them, and to know how to behave based on them is the key to becoming an emotionally intelligent person. And it is as necessary to good relationships as food is to living.

Learning about our feelings is the first step toward keeping the tail from wagging the dog and putting the dog back in control. But that's just an analogy. I am not relating you to a dog. I like dogs very much; they are cute and like me back. So once again, please, no hate mail.

When the tail wags the dog, it looks silly.

MISERABLE TEENAGERS

You know what a funny fruit is? The apple. It's very beneficial for you in a lot of ways. Not only does it have more vitamin C than an orange, but it also works better than coffee if you need a pick-me-up. When you eat an apple, it takes a lot to digest it, and the enzymes that your body uses to do that cause you to wake up and have a lot more energy. So next time you want to buy a five-dollar latte drink, pick up an apple instead. But be careful; the skin of the apple is the least beneficial. It actually has small traces of the poison cyanide in it. So don't eat two hundred apple skins—even if someone bets you money that you can't.[1]

In addition to being good for you, apples have had a lot to do with love, truth, misery, and happiness throughout history. Apples were commonly used to help people identify love and a future spouse. It's said that an unmarried girl can discover her future husband by peeling the skin from an apple in one piece and throwing it over her left shoulder. If the peel forms a letter, then that letter will be the first initial of the name of the guy she will marry.

This seems like a foolproof way to make relationship decisions, if you ask me. Well . . . if you want to be miserable, that is. In fact, a lot of people do some pretty silly things that end up making them more unhappy than happy.

▶ Pay Attention

I like guitar. But then again, how many people hate guitar? Right. So I like guitar. Anyway, I've played for a long time, and I like to go see lots of shows. I currently live in Nashville, and there's a lot of talent. My friend told me of an eighteen- or nineteen-year-old phenom guitar player from Australia. So we went to see him early one evening. He is a gangly, skinny, sweet-looking kid. Of course, having an Aussie accent in the States doesn't hurt his chances with the ladies. We sat right up front in a small room with probably a hundred people in it. Then the kid went to work. *Ummm . . . what is happening?!?* was my actual first thought after about thirteen seconds of watching him play. I've been playing about fifteen years, and I can't even begin to touch on some of the things this kid was doing effortlessly in his teens.

But then, I got weird, like I do sometimes.

The first thirty seconds or so is actually all I watched of the guitar stuff, because I got distracted by a guitar cord for the next forty-five minutes. You know the little cord that plugs into a guitar and then into the amplifier? That one. The young, crazy guitar kid kept walking from side to side on the small stage. But he didn't trip over the guitar cord. Not once. And he should have. I seriously watched the cord and then his feet for almost forty-five minutes. I missed the entire show because I was staring at a stupid cord.

I tried to do some calculations on the odds of him *not* tripping over the cord, and I still can't explain it. There were probably at least sixty to seventy times that he came within less than an inch of tripping over that cord. He would be looking up at the crowd and playing ridiculous notes and riffs and all the while skipping around and missing that cord by a fraction of space, not even noticing that he almost ate it into a drum set and amplifier about a hundred times. Which would have probably changed the mood of the show.

Here's what I concluded. Even though he may not have been looking at the guitar cord, he was aware that it was there, and so his behavior adapted to it, even if it was only on a subconscious level. It's the only explanation I can think of.

And why would I tell you this little tidbit of a story? Because it has to do with behavior. It's kind of my blessing and curse: I pay attention to behavior. I observe it obsessively, dissect it, and try to make sense of it. Sometimes it distracts me, but it also has helped me to make sense of a lot of things, especially for young people. Turns out that when you pay attention to behavior, you can learn an awful lot.

Now all we have to do is apply that understanding of behavior to issues in your life. Like being happy versus being miserable. Super easy right?

Turns out that when you pay attention to behavior, you can learn an awful lot.

What Makes Us Happy or Miserable?

Here are some things that make me happy:

- puppies

- the air of the Pacific Northwest

smiles

 seeing a new, faraway place

 thinking about new colors

 sitting on the porch with my friends

 kissing

 feeling free

 feeling responsible

 helping other people

Now, what makes you happy? Make a list. You can probably do this pretty easily.

_____

_____

_____

_____

I know it seems kind of weird to make a list of things that can make me miserable, but here are a few:

 traffic

 chewing food with your mouth open

lying

sitting for too long

bad music

but mostly, myself

Turns out, I am the key to making myself miserable or not miserable. That's what I have learned. I actually do have patience, but I can choose to throw it out the window. I can choose to be understanding, or I can close my mind. I can choose to enjoy moments when I'm sitting with others, or I can become self-centered. And that's just the start. How I look at my friends, the opportunities I have in life, my job, the things that I have to get done—these don't determine whether or not I am happy. It's not the *things*; it's me.

How about you? Do you ever wonder if it is what's happening in your life or simply your mind-set about it that makes you miserable? Do you have miserable friends? For example:

Chad,

I feel so miserable all of the time! All I want is to have friends and be happy and be in love, but I am always miserable! Help! I try everything. I go to church, and I try to do everything that I can for people. Guys don't seem interested in me. Nothing I do ever works, and I'm sick of it. Some people are just happy, and some people are just miserable. I'm thinking I'm just one of the miserable ones, and I don't know what to do about it. But I'm sick and tired of it.

—Miserable

Sometimes people don't see the problems in their lives until they are staring right at them, square in the nose. I wish that more people, myself included, would take constant inventory and evaluate what's going on in their lives. But they don't. They wait until a crisis occurs before they ever even look at the situation from other angles, angles larger than themselves. Much of being miserable isn't just fate. A lot of it has to do with our choices and our behaviors.

What do you think makes some people so miserable? Jot down some ideas.

_____

_____

_____

_____

_____

_____

How about you? What are some things that make you miserable?

_____

_____

_____

_____

Look at those two lists. The things that can make you miserable are often the things you can't control. Let's be honest. A terrible family life makes things difficult. If you are missing a parent, or don't feel loved, or don't have people to talk to, then life is automatically more difficult. It's just a fact. But it doesn't have to determine the outcome of your life; it doesn't mean that life has to be awful. I know many people—myself included—who have personally come from awful backgrounds and family circumstances to lead happy lives, full of promise. It's a process, but it starts with a decision. But before we jump to that, let's get to some of the stuff that seems to suck the happiness out of people.

A man's as
miserable as he
thinks he is.

—Seneca,
Roman Philosopher

Emotional Monsters

If your emotions lead you around like a dog on a leash, you're going to get dragged around a lot. And you'll get a lot of bumps, bruises, and scars to show for it. Emotions are wonderful. They are necessary. They are what make us so human, so beautiful, so vulnerable, so mysterious. They can also be a torture device, especially if they are the only thing controlling you.

I was at a dinner with some author friends of mine talking over a new book project, and out of nowhere they asked me a strange question: "Chad, what do you think about people and how they make decisions? What does that say about them?" Whoa, I mean, that's right up there with, "What do you think about life?" So I thought about it for a minute while I was eating some weird pastry with meat in it, and then a thought came to mind. I said I thought that people who always make decisions based on emotion seem to be the most unhappy. In other words, people who just feel their way through *everything* often seem to be very miserable. I don't know if that's true for everyone, but it's true for all of the people I have known.

> *People who always make decisions based on emotion seem to be the most unhappy.*

Even though feelings are great, they also lie, mislead, and even attack. We'll chat about this subject some more later, but for now let's just say that everyone has emotions, and some of us have emotional monsters on our backs. And they're weighing us down.

Over the years, counselors, researchers, and people like me have noticed some common mind-sets and behaviors in young people who are unsatisfied with their lives. Do any of these sound like you?

Fear of Everything

There's only one thing you can be certain of, and that is that you don't know what's going to happen. This uncertainty sets some people free, but it paralyzes others. Maybe you are afraid that nothing will work out for you. Perhaps it's that people won't like you, or you don't even know how to "be" with people. Maybe it's a fear that people are going to abandon you, or hurt you in ways that you have been hurt before. Fear keeps you stuck in life; it hurts you by keeping you from fully living.

Some people would rather be certain they're miserable, than risk being happy.

—Dr. Robert Anthony

Fear of the Past

Instead of looking to the future, some people are shackled to their pasts. Their past experiences, their former feelings, their old habits, their old mind-sets. Change is hard. But get this in your head: Every single human being has screwed up many, many times. You can either stay chained to your mistakes and relive and repeat them, *or* you can learn from them and make better and smarter choices. The fear of the past can ruin your future. Everyone has a past, and we have to work through it to a better future. You can try it on your own. You can try willpower, discipline, talking it out. But I'm firmly convinced that relationships are the things that make us want to change and grow, and I have always found that a relationship with God is a pillar of strength to lean on when we don't have enough strength on our own. I've found a lot of truth in my own life on that one. I promise I'm no better than you, I'm just telling you what has helped me and many others.

Isolation

Sometimes I like to be alone, and sometimes I need to be alone. We all do. But sometimes being alone is the worst thing I can do for myself and others. We are made to be with people. Sometimes I get tired of hearing overused church words like "community" and "fellowship," mainly because they seem cheesy and old. But their basic, core meaning is true. We need people, and we don't exist well without them. C. S. Lewis once described hell as a neighborhood where everything looked perfect, except everyone lived in different houses, isolated from one another, not knowing or talking to their neighbors, completely separated from anyone else's life.[2] Hell was isolation from one another and isolation from God. And that kind of scared me.

Teens who isolate themselves suffer. They are more likely to be depressed, to try to hurt themselves, and to suffer social setbacks. They have poorer skills in communication, interacting with other people, and relationships. We are simply not made to be alone.

I'm gonna Bible verse you on this one: "Forgetting what is behind and straining toward what is ahead, I press on toward the goal to win the prize for which God has called me heavenward in Christ Jesus."

—Philippians 3:13–14 NIV

Focusing on Relationships with the Opposite Sex

Blah blah blah. I'm sure you've heard this before. Doesn't mean it's not true. I'm not telling you what to do or not do; I'm telling you the things that miserable teenagers do. Although it's great to learn about how to be in relationships, the people who always cling to the opposite sex and set their freaky tractor beam on "obsess and hunt" will find that these relationships don't satisfy; they confuse.

Relationships have to be balanced, just like everything else in your life. Even the most appealing things. If you have a bowl of chocolate sitting next to a well-balanced, healthy meal, I'm sure a young kid would dig right into the chocolate and skip the meal, because chocolate is way more exciting. But it would leave him sick and malnourished—and probably gassy. And he could feed it to the dog and kill it. (Side note: Dogs should not eat chocolate.) The same is true of relationships. You need to have a well-balanced "diet" of family, friends, and the opposite sex. When it comes to dating relationships, people end up having much better relationships when they keep every other part of their lives in balance: God, family, friends, significant other, hobbies, school, work, and so on.

Being the "Maker Fun-er-of-er"

This is a weird one, but bear with me. Think of the sarcastic person who always pokes fun at or indirectly puts people down. Sometimes that person is just trying to be funny, or maybe he or she is clueless. Either way, these people tend to spread negativity, which is a form of misery, especially in high school.

If you aren't building people up, there is a good chance that you are helping break them down, sometimes without knowing it. I know this because I've struggled with being sarcastic, not realizing how negative I'm being. But it brings people down, and it eventually brings me down. Sarcastic people are usually unhappy themselves, and when left to their own devices, they start to feel the burden of negativity that they are placing on others. So don't be fooled. You are always either building others up or breaking them down.

Captain Embarrass You

Again, this person might look like he is in control, but tearing others down will make him—or you, if you are that person—unhappy. I've said it before: no one likes to be embarrassed, especially girls when they are in public. But plenty of girls will run their mouths off and embarrass people too. In some confused sense of independence and confidence, they often believe they can say anything that comes to mind because it makes them feel so bold.

Many times, we aren't taught to be empathetic and sensitive to others. And when we aren't, we cause others to become a little more miserable. But when we do choose to be sensitive to others, we make people feel loved. Then we, in turn, feel more love because we are doing something good. Don't embarrass people. It might seem funny at the time, but behind the smile there is the sting like a small, sharp knife through the heart.

Refusing to Listen

If you don't listen to people, or don't bother to learn how to listen, you will become more egocentric, self-centered, and ultimately more unhappy. Most people aren't born with the ability to listen well. Just as people have to learn to drive, they have to learn to be good listeners. When you learn to listen to others, you focus less on yourself in a healthy way. And when you open up your heart and take an interest in other people's words and lives, your brain releases chemicals like dopamine and oxytocin that help you feel happier and closer to people, and therefore less miserable. Try it. Listening is powerful, it is good, and it is needed in every relationship that you can possibly think of. Also, everyone loves a good listener, and it makes you much more attractive to people. But that should just be a perk.

Whining

Want some cheese with your whine?

Whiners are people who are never satisfied. They grumble and complain about everything and everyone, and guess what? It's annoying! And it can also be a self-fulfilling prophecy. If you expect bad things to happen, then you will probably find that bad things happen in your life.

No one wants to hang around someone who whines. It's stressful, and people will find a way to avoid you. So practice being positive. It will make you happier, and people won't avoid you. And a positive outlook also can be a self-fulfilling prophecy. Expect good, and find good. Being positive is just better in every conceivable way.

Expect good, and find good.

Being Mr. Macho Guy or Miss Macho Girl

This goes for both guys and girls. They put up walls to keep everything and everyone out. They pretend they don't really care about anyone or anything. They isolate their true selves and show the world a fake person, appearing to be strong and confident. But real strength and confidence aren't an act. They come from being comfortable in your own skin. Don't put on some borrowed image of who you think you should be—people don't like that. Acting as if you don't care or that you are too tough shows a lack of humanity. Nothing will make you miserable inside faster than separating yourself from humanity.

Static-Cling Humans

Do you stick to things or to people too much? Then you might need some human static remover. Spray it on and get off of other people, especially the people you might be smothering with your clinginess and not even know it. You are being unbalanced, and it will make you—and those around you—unhappy. One person cannot possibly meet all your needs, and it's wrong to expect him to. Obsession will not only drive people away, but it will also make you even more frantic and desperate when you don't find what you're looking for.

So don't be human static cling. Guys like balance and a little mystery in girls, and I know you girls like that too. So put some dryer sheets on yourself and get rid of that cling!

I Am Superior

Miserable people often act superior, but it's just an act. Inside, they are insecure and hurting. Happy, healthy people don't feel the need to put themselves above other people. An emotionally healthy person doesn't want others to feel smaller, because there is absolutely nothing good that comes from that. People who have to brag and one-up others all the time can't be excited for other people, because they need those people to be excited for them. This is selfish and annoying. And even if it impresses some people in high school, I promise it ends the day you graduate. People wise up, and they find that behavior super-duper stupid. Happy people want others to feel better about themselves, more loved, more capable.

Miserable, lost, hurting people take from others to make themselves feel bigger or better. Don't be confused by that behavior. It's a lie.

Swapping God for People

I don't know if you believe in God or not. But if you do, there are times that people decide to leave him behind for a little while and go look for other things that they think will be more satisfying. Sure, God is hard to ask out on a date, and you don't look at him and get butterflies in your stomach and hope that he wants to hold your hand at the movies. I can see why people or other flashy interests can seem more appealing at times, especially with all those dumb hormones that give you zits and make you crazy. But if you have decided to make God a priority in your life, it takes time to learn how to do that.

If you make guys or girls your first priority, if you try to put them in that number one spot where God should be, you will find the outcome to be confusing and not so great. It's like water. If you switch from drinking pure water to anything else—even if it has lots of taste and fake sugar—your body will suffer. In the same way, if you switch from nourishing your heart and soul with God to anything else—no matter how hot he or she is or how many butterflies you get—your heart and soul will suffer. God promises to be the pure spiritual water that we need. He never leaves, he never decides someone else is cooler or cuter, and he always loves you. Also, high-fructose corn syrup is awful for you. Don't argue. It's just a fact. Nitrous, power-bomb sugar drinks are dumb. Take that, non-real energy drinks.

Changing Human Beings Besides Yourself

Even if you could change a guy or a girl, it's not your job. You aren't a parent, so don't take on that role. And it's generally not a good idea to get into a relationship unless you appreciate that person for who he or she is right now. If a person changes because of your influence, that's one thing, but to set out to change someone is not a great start for a relationship. You can't force someone to change. It's more likely that you will end up doing the changing, and usually not for the better.

Love Me, Love Me, Love Me, Please???

I can't say this enough. Love must be freely given. It's one of the hardest truths to accept, but you'll just have to take my word for it. You can't force it, you can't hold on to it and squeeze it, and you can't just create it because you want it.

I can't "make" people like me. I just have to be me, and maybe they'll like me, maybe they won't. I mean, some people love my books, and some people tell me I'm dumb and I'm not funny and everything I do is nonsense. Believe me, you can't make people *like* you, so why would you try to make them *love* you? The more you push something on someone, the likelier he or she is to reject it. Like it or not, there is a natural order to the roles of chase-ee and chaser, and they both have to want to play the game. If you chase and the other person doesn't want you to, then you are a stalker. Sorry. Don't do that.

People Pleasers

As strange as it is, the people who want to make other people happy all the time often find themselves feeling miserable. You can't make yourself happy by simply making others feel happy. I'm a bit of a people pleaser myself, and I want others to be happy, but I always do it on my terms. I usually pick the way that I think will make them happy, and oftentimes I'm wrong.

Happy, healthy people don't try to please everyone, because it can't be done. It's an illusion. You can be kind, gracious, giving, but you can't make others like you just by the things you do for them. You'll get taken advantage of, you'll have your fuel tank drained, you'll end up empty, and you'll suffer miserably. Learn the word "no." It's a healthy balancer, and everyone needs to learn to use it confidently, even on themselves. Learn to care and be cared about; don't run around trying to please everyone into loving you. That's just out of whack.

Relationship Pros

Doing something a lot doesn't mean that you are doing it right. In fact, the classic definition for insanity is doing something over and over again and expecting a different result. But people do this all the time with dating, and it usually leaves them miserable—and probably a little insane.

I hate to be the party pooper, but there aren't really any benefits to getting into relationships at a young age. I've said it thousands of times, but I am telling you again because it is so important. There are *lots* of benefits to having *lots* of friends, but dating is something entirely different. Part of dating well comes with age and learning how to deal with the emotions of your heart. Ask anyone who dated lots and lots when they were young. Almost all of them will tell you that they wish they had spent more time understanding themselves and less time running around worrying about love.

Spending your youth being youthful is better than racking up relationship numbers. And people who tell you to run out into the world with your heart wide-open are putting a target on your heart. Tell them not to do that, and that I said so.

Relationship Jumpers

Relationships are not a series of trampolines for you to jump from one to another to another. If you jump directly from one relationship to the next, then you are likely going to have more emotional baggage, more problems, and more self-confusion. You try to avoid pain by transferring it into a focus on the next relationship, but you become an emotional ticking time bomb. In addition to being just plain miserable, you put yourself at a much higher risk for depression, emotional pain, poor self-esteem, disease, sexual abuse, not to mention a broken heart. If you find yourself stuck in this cycle, take a break, throw off the things that distract you, and set your eyes on things that are constant. God said a few thousand things about that. People are not constants in life. God is. Just FYI.

> The LORD is my rock, my fortress and my deliverer; my God is my rock, in whom I take refuge, my shield and the horn of my salvation, my stronghold.
>
> —Psalm 18:2 NIV

Live for Today, and Only Today

You don't have to know your future; you can't anyway. But if your vision of the future only exists in today, well, you might find that things will get foggy on you, and you won't be able to figure out why you aren't headed anywhere purposeful. And that will make you more likely to be miserable.

People adopt a lot of sayings about living for the moment, like: "Live for today; it's all you have," "No regrets. Do what you want and learn from it," and "My mistakes and imperfections make me better." Sorry, but these are not philosophies. They are short-sightedness, and they will do nothing for you except make each day more confusing.

You can enjoy each day while still keeping in mind that tomorrow will be affected by your decisions today, because it will be. If tomorrow didn't matter at all, I would do a lot of weird stuff probably involving shooting some signs with a shotgun, spearing some fish at the aquarium, and maybe running around downtown with war paint all over my face and trying to ride a wild horse. But if it turned out to not really be my last day, that next day would sure be awkward. And odds are that I'd have some pretty expensive tickets to pay.

What I'm trying to say is that you can enjoy the present while still thinking and planning for the future. Enjoy where you are, but know where you are going. No one really knows if there will be a tomorrow, but that doesn't mean God wants us to live in fear or make silly mistakes because we're not thinking past today.

When people don't look to the future at all, they have the potential to (a) do dumb/awesome things, like riding wild horses in public places, wearing war paint and destroying important signage. So I've heard anyway. Or, (b) live complacent lives and not reach their potential.

If you can learn to live each day making good use of your relationships, your time and resources, and the gifts God gave you, not only will you live a life of no regrets today, but you will also give God the opportunity to do awesome things with your future.

Impersonating Jell-O

So many people, often miserable people, become human Jell-O, molding and changing for those around them. They think it will make others like them, though that's a lie in the end. They end up feeling ashamed and angry because they don't know how to just be themselves. It happens to almost all of us at some point. But if there is one thing that people appreciate, it is people who do not try to mold themselves into what they think other people want. So for your sake—eat Jell-O; don't be Jell-O.

Eat Jell-O; don't be Jell-O.

Giving to Get Love

This is kind of a weird and hard but true thing. So many people try to earn their way into someone's heart.

Chad,

Help me know what to do about something. There's a guy and he's nice, but he overdoes it. He writes me notes all the time, he sends me flowers, he calls my house and comments on everything I do on Facebook. He is really nice, but it's like way too much. There was part of me that might have been interested in him, but now it just seems odd, and I don't think I would like someone who likes me too much. He says he knows me, but he really doesn't. I don't like that. How should I deal with it?

—Jamie

Again, you can't force people to like you, let alone love you. And if you push unequally, you'll be creepy. I know you aren't creepy, but other people might think you are. And this goes for girls, as well as guys. You cannot just give your love and then demand that the other person love you in return. Love has to be given equally and by both parties at a time when their hearts are both looking for the same thing.

Secret Miseries

If you are like most human beings, there are things about yourself that only you know. Maybe you were abused, or are being abused. Maybe you hurt yourself. Maybe you just have a hard time comparing yourself to others. Maybe you're struggling with sexual addiction or the shame of pornography. Perhaps you don't know your mom or your dad. Maybe no one has ever understood you. But if you look at the person next to you—no matter who it is—I can guarantee you one thing: that person is hiding things too. Everyone does. And hidden things are the cancer of the soul. They don't go away because we run away, dig holes, bury them, and throw away the map. They always find their way out. And yet I want you to know that God is there to forgive and heal those secrets. I don't just preach this. After trying every other method of dealing with secret miseries, I'm finding it's true in my own life

If you ever need help, check out these resources. You are worth it.

The Revolve Tour at *www.revolvetour.com*

Defender Ministries at *www.defenderministries.com*

Pure Life Ministries at *www.purelifeministries.org/free-resources*

New Life Ministries at *http://newlife.com*

The Deceptive Qualities

People are complex. One of the many reasons that people experience misery in life is because they have an unrealistic outlook about people. And sooner or later, it will let them down. I'm not just talking about thinking you'll find the perfect guy or girl, and he or she will make everything great. I am talking about the qualities that we can become fixated on that will only disappoint. For example, it's natural to want to find someone cute and physically attractive. But what happens when people become fixated on only the hot guys or girls? They throw the other qualities—like kindness, compassion, and respect—to the wayside and fixate on the superficial. The cocky guy who seems confident, the pretty girl who thinks only of herself, the super youth group leader who worships himself as much as God, the wealthy kid with lots of friends who promises new opportunities for you—these things can be attractive at first, but they are a false promise, and they can really bite you later. Step back and look at your relationships with a bigger set of lenses that can look further into people and a little further into the future too.

Performing for the Audience of None

So many times people live as though there is an audience or a panel of judges watching their every move. I get it. It's pretty natural to behave with other people in mind. I've done it plenty of times before. The people who usually say they don't care what anyone thinks are the people who care the most. I mean, why waste your time with that sentence if you don't care? But one key to being miserable is to perform and dance and jingle as though there were some panel of people constantly judging you. These people are ghosts. They aren't even really there, and yet we dance and sing for them all the time.

The people who usually say they don't care what anyone thinks are the people who care the most. I mean, why waste your time with that sentence if you don't care?

It's good to be aware of other people and how they see us. But it's not good to live our lives for them. There is a huge difference. I hope you will consider God the person that you perform and live your life for. He is there to encourage you, not simply give you a score. He's your number one fan.

There are plenty of reasons to be miserable, but there are also plenty of reasons to choose hope and peace, no matter what your circumstances are. Miserable is a choice. People choose it, but they don't have to. And I hope you won't. There is too much beauty in this life to just ignore it. All we have to do is open our eyes to it.

Everything can be taken from a man but one thing: the last of the human freedoms—to choose one's attitude in any given set of circumstances, to choose one's own way.

—Victor Frankl

10

HAPPY TEENAGERS

Do you know who lives in igloos, and where? Probably Eskimos, and in Alaska, right? Actually, no. Most likely no one lives in them anymore. The word itself—*igloo*—means "house" in Inuit. And most igloos were not made of snow blocks; they were made of stone or hide. Although we all have a pretty picture in our minds of little people in whale hides living in igloos with spears and little kayaks, it's just not true.

Igloos made of snow are completely unknown in Alaska. They were only used by Canadian Eskimos at one point in history, and few, if any, remain today. It wasn't until the 1920s that a Denver newspaper erected a snow igloo near where some reindeer were kept and hired an Alaskan Eskimo to tell the visitors that he and the other people lived in houses like that in Alaska. In fact, he himself had never seen one before except in the movies.[1]

There are so many mythical things that we have been led to believe, like Santa Claus, the Tooth Fairy, Eskimos in igloos, and other various urban legends. (Also, Columbus didn't discover America. And he was a bad dude. Sorry.) But like many of these myths we have been led to believe, they simply aren't true.

There's one more myth: all teens struggle. But in fact, that's just not the case. Teens do great things. Happiness and joy fill their lives. But our media, our TV shows, our sources of information all thrive on the suffering, drama, and mistakes of human beings.

Yeah, some teens suffer. But there are also many, many happy teenagers out there. I hope you are one, and if not, there might be some notes we can take from those who are.

Teens do great things.

▶▶ How to Make Teens Happy . . . Really?

I once read an article called "How to Make a Teenager Happy." I thought, *Wow, it's cool that someone figured it out. Let's see what they have to say.* So here was the entire secret for how to make you happy, written from an adult's perspective. I think it covers every single base. Okay, I might be a little sarcastic about it.

> One of the best and easiest ways to make [teenagers] happy is to let them have some fun. Let them get their way once in a while. . . . At this stage in life they do not want you to be parents, they want you to be more [like] their friends that do what they like to do.

The three gems of wisdom were as follows:

1. Sit down with your teenager and have a discussion about things they want to do that will help make them happy.
2. Have them do their responsibilities first, such as cleaning, doing what is asked of them by parents or family members, homework. Their responsibilities are a must before any extra activities. This should be done with respect and without any hassle.

3. Once everything that is expected of them is done and you both have come to some kind of agreement on things that are allowed, let them go have fun.[2]

Now that we have that cleared up, I'm sure you have all the answers you need, right? If you sit down with your parents and talk about things that make you happy, do your chores, and go have fun, you'll be perfect. Got it? Right. Don't you just love generic formulas for life? Of course, it's well-intentioned, but it doesn't cover the complex dimensions of your life, or anyone else's. Although doing your chores is important, it's not what brings happiness to people. People need more than that. Now go take out the trash.

What REALLY Makes Teens Happy

In the last chapter, we talked a lot about the things and the decisions that help make people, specifically teenagers, unhappy and often miserable, but what about the opposite? What are the things that make people happy?

One of the largest—if not *the* largest and most extensive and expensive—research projects on happiness was done by Dr. Martin Seligman, and it was documented in a book called *Authentic Happiness.* It tried to uncover some of the secrets to happiness. While I, as well as Dr. Seligman, don't think that God can be excluded as the final part of this equation, there is still a lot of great information in his research.

Very simply, we look to be happy and to be fulfilled our whole lives. Some ways work; others don't. Some of Dr. Seligman's findings that I thought were interesting are these:

☆ Happiness comes from the exercise of kindness more easily than it does from searching out fun.

☆ My loneliest times are the times that I am solely concerned with myself, my needs, and my desires.

☆ The belief that we can rely on shortcuts to happiness, joy, or ecstasy, rather than finding them by the exercise of personal strengths and virtues, leads to a great number of spiritually starving people.

☆ Trying to just be positive without a lifestyle and habits with character leads to emptiness, to inauthenticity, and even to depression.

☆ The six core virtues that were noted for those who experience happiness are wisdom and knowledge, courage, love and humility, justice, temperance, and spirituality (and in my opinion, that's also perfectly in line with the spiritual encounter of Jesus).[3]

The best way to cheer yourself up is to try to cheer somebody else up.

—Mark Twain

*Focusing on fulfillment in relationships,
money, and people doesn't lead to happiness.*

There is a lot more that I won't bore you with, and I hope those words don't sound too big or adult-ish to think about. But I will tell you that focusing on fulfillment in relationships, money, and people doesn't lead to happiness. You have to have something deeper in your foundation.

Learning to be Happy

Okay, Chad's going to be vulnerable again. This is new to me too. LOL. I must say that this happy thing is something I'm still learning about. I have always thought of myself as a pretty happy person. I try to be. But there are a lot of things I've experienced that have negatively affected me, and I didn't even know that they were a problem. I thought that my upbringing in a broken family, like so many others, didn't affect me as much as it did. After all, a lot of other people have had it much worse. I thought that being alone most of my life made me more independent. I thought that my criticism of things was because I saw them as capable of being better. I thought that I had a lot of patience, because in some ways with some people, I do. But I have found that a lot of the things I had been telling myself didn't affect me were actually coming out in my life in ways I didn't know. I can crack a joke and laugh with the best of them. I know I have a good sense of humor and that others appreciate it. But I can also have a lot of impatience, sarcasm, and cynicism.

I was back in Alaska recently, hanging out at a camp with some counselors. We sat in a room with the windows open, overlooking the green fields and horse pastures, with the ocean a few hundred yards away and the snowcapped mountains looking back at us in the distance. It's a nice way to start the morning. Each day I spent a couple of hours with them, talking about the future. We talked about the things that they wanted to do. I asked them what they were good at. I asked them about their strengths, their virtues, their talents, and their passions. Surprisingly, a lot of them had never really thought about what made them so great, or they were too reluctant to say it. And then one of the counselors, a kind and very unique young lady, told the group something that was good about herself. She said that there was always something inside of her that couldn't help but love everybody. She said her heart has always been so full of love and compassion for people that she can't contain it. And you know what? She meant it. I watched her, and her statement was a truth in action. She loved people all the time, and she couldn't help it. I get angry about slow traffic.

I went for a long walk and cried. Why couldn't I do that? Instead of getting impatient with people, why couldn't I just love people, no matter how odd or hard to love they are? Why does my heart get blocked? I went to a smoldering campfire and got down on my knees. It smelled like cedar, and it was a much-needed weak moment that I am thankful for. I asked the Lord to forgive me. I asked him to take away the blockage in my heart that keeps love from flowing. I asked him to help me stop trying to figure things out on my own, and to let go of myself and be filled with him. I asked for patience and wisdom and humility.

If any of you lacks wisdom, he should ask God, who gives generously to all without finding fault, and it will be given to him.

—James 1:5 NIV

Slowly, in the right amounts, he is giving it to me. Because my friend shared her love for others, I wanted to be filled up with that same love. And I'll tell you something that I can't explain. Since that day, I haven't cared to be sarcastic. I haven't once wanted to make a joke that might make someone feel uncomfortable. My patience keeps growing. I want my friends and family to know how much I love them. And I don't think I'll ever be able to explain it. I have tried so hard to make myself happy in so many ways, but I was shipwrecking myself on an island of loneliness. I'm learning that happiness comes in sharing joy and love with other people and letting them share it with you. I don't know how to break that down into "Five Quick & Easy Steps to Happiness," but I wanted you to know that I'm on the same search for truth and happiness as you. We are all on it together.

Our culture has spent the greater part of the last century trying to figure out what's wrong with us young people. They spent more time looking for what is wrong with us than what is right with us. We know all about the things that make us miserable: broken relationships, heartache, diseases, psychological disorders, alcoholism, addiction, low self-esteem. But what are the things that make us right? From a Christian perspective, God is obviously the big answer. But we shouldn't just say "God" and act like nothing else ever matters. There are other things too, daily things, small things, people, habits, and choices that make life more enjoyable—or much harder.

Choose a Positive Attitude

For starters, people who are happy *choose* to be optimistic. Yes, it starts with a choice. It's a behavioral and mental and emotional choice to look at things positively and choose to latch onto the things that are positive instead of focusing on the negative. There are both positives and negatives in any circumstance; it's what we choose to hang onto that determines our long-term outlook in life. For example, being active is one of the simplest things that makes people of all ages happy. When dogs sit still and lie around all day, they get sick and live shorter lives. They are not meant to do that; they are meant to run and play and be dogs. While we are not basset hounds, we share some common traits. Healthiness, happiness, and longevity are directly related to how much we "play," how much activity we have in our lives. If you sit and watch TV or just drive around or play video games, odds are that you will experience less happiness in your life than if you were more active.

Most folks are
about as happy
as they make up
their minds to be.

—Abraham
Lincoln

A long-term study of almost three thousand people showed that those who were more active and optimistic were half as likely to die as others their age. They were also half as likely to get sick and become disabled. The renowned Mayo Clinic has proven that optimists live significantly longer than pessimists. People who choose to be optimists also have better health habits, lower blood pressure, and healthier immune systems. Everyone knows being happy is important—and it's definitely more fun—but it also helps you live longer and healthier lives.[4]

I don't know about you, but I hear a lot about how teenagers do things wrong. And I'm sure it is helpful to see our errors, but so is knowing how to do things right. In fact, I can watch someone swing a tennis racket wrong all day, and it won't teach me a thing about how to do it right. I need someone to show me, and then I need to practice. The same thing is true for happiness. We need to see happiness and learn about it before we just understand how to be great and smiley and neato all day.

Body Image

Just shape up at the gym and get that toned, hairless, ripped body—then you'll be happy and love yourself. Oops. You are wrong. It turns out that physical attractiveness will not make you happier. I'm sorry. Although it can help you feel better about yourself, and although there are advantages for people who are physically attractive, there is no statistical evidence that it has any real bearing on your happiness.

I always say, "Get comfortable in your own skin." I try to live by my own advice, and it's easier said than done, but it's worth trying. People who accept themselves and appreciate their physical attributes are better off than the prettiest people who invest their happiness only in their exterior. It might sound cliché, but the evidence and personal testimonies don't lie. I have met some of the prettiest girls and best-looking guys who hated themselves. There is no set judge of beauty. It can be yourself or other people. Frankly, I wouldn't leave it to them. A lot of people don't see things very clearly. And they might need glasses.

Get comfortable in your own skin.

Not Having Sex Will Make You Happier

Babies are neat, but not when you are a teenager, and not when you are a single parent. Most teen relationships that involve sex end less than four weeks after they start having sex. Most teens, more than 80 percent of girls and more than 60 percent of guys, say they regret having sex.[5] That's the unhappy part.

The happy part is that teens who don't have sex have less regrets, generally show better grades, and have better friendships, family relationships, and physical and emotional health. If you want to be happier, keep your pants on. Sex is good, but it is a warm fire that needs a solid foundation. This happens in loving, committed marriages. When it doesn't have that foundation, it usually burns up the things—and the people—around it.

> *If you want to be happier,*
> *keep your pants on.*

Dating, Schmating

Teens who take dating less seriously, or who don't involve themselves in it, are happier. I'm not demonizing dating; I'm just telling you that it won't bring you the happiness and fulfillment that you may be expecting. It might for some, especially when it's done right, when they treat it as a learning experience and don't become sexually active. But people have trouble balancing it and putting boundaries around it. They dive headfirst, right into the shallow end of the kiddie pool. And they hurt themselves, sometimes very badly.

> *Some people just forget that they have hope,*
> *no matter what they face.*

▶▶ Real, Live Happy Teenagers

I have interviewed teenagers who describe themselves as happy and content. Their answers were interesting. I'll give you an example of one of the interviews that represented the "happy" kids pretty well.

CHAD: Would you describe yourself as someone who is happy with life most of the time, or unhappy with life most of the time? Can you give an estimated percentage?

BAILEY: I'm mostly happy, 75 to 80 percent of the time.

CHAD: Have you always been a happy person? Do you think that it is more because of your circumstances or an attitude you were born with?

BAILEY: Both. Good parents play a part. But I'm not sure completely. You have to choose to be happy. Some people just forget that they have hope, no matter what they face. As a Christian, I know that I have hope in the future and that it's bigger than just my circumstances that I face.

CHAD: What is the point of dating?

BAILEY: I think that you date to find different qualities in people that you like or don't like. But I think you have to be careful with it, and not to act on what your emotions are telling you, 'cause those suckers can drive me wild. My mom taught me that.

CHAD: Do you date? And at what age did you start dating?

BAILEY: Yes, I have dated. The first person I dated was in tenth grade. I think that I didn't know how to do it though, and it caused me some heartache. I wish I would have waited at least another year or so.

CHAD: What are some of the habits of unhealthy or miserable kids that you see? Why do you think they feel that way?

BAILEY: I think circumstances, mainly family circumstances, play a big part, like it or not. I think if you have a close, healthy family, then you are learning how to deal with life and the hard parts. And if you don't have that, you just don't quite know what to do. And that makes me sad, I guess, but I think it's true.

CHAD: What is love? Your definition?

BAILEY: I think love is something that you have to act out before you can say it.

CHAD: Hey, are you ripping me off? I feel like I said that once and you stole it.

BAILEY: What?!?

CHAD: Never mind. Moving on.

CHAD: How many people do you think you should date before getting married?

BAILEY: I dunno. I'm going to guess maybe five? I guess to experience different people and different characteristics. Maybe just to know different things about different people.

CHAD: Why do you think that some kids try to disengage from their family and other kids get along well with their family?

BAILEY: Probably parenting style. I have a good relationship with my parents, so I like to spend time with them. A lot of people think that it's weird to want to spend time with your family, but I like my family, so it's strange to hear that from people.

CHAD: Since you like your family, what is a favorite quality about your parents?

BAILEY: They are pretty real. They don't sugarcoat things in life. They are honest, and they care about me.

CHAD: What are some of your habits that have kept you positive, happy, and optimistic?

BAILEY: Probably a few things. I'm involved in a lot of sports, and I like to be busy. And honestly, some people might not get this, but the Bible. I think it renews my mind each day. I have tried to make reading it a habit and, personally, it helps me.

CHAD: Have you been unhappy or miserable during any phases of your life? Can you think of some of the characteristics of why you were miserable?

BAILEY: Yeah, I was miserable for a while, mostly because of friend circumstances. I grew up with two girlfriends my whole life, and they moved away in the same month. And then girls started to get competitive at school when I was a freshman, and I felt very alone.

CHAD: What is the happiest time of your life so far? Can you think of a couple reasons why it seemed or seems like the best?

BAILEY: Graduating high school. I just graduated. It felt like a good accomplishment. And because I'm excited about college. I loved high school, but I'm pretty pumped for the fall and being a freshman all over again! And I want to live in a dorm! I've always looked forward to living the college life. You can tell I'm pumped, right?

CHAD: Yes, I can. You are getting very squiggly, and your voice just went up about five steps.

Which brings me to my next point: What are the things that happy people do?

➡️ **Things Happy People Do**

Happy People Think about Their Future

When you think about your future, you are doing all kinds of things to your brain and your heart and your body that you don't understand. There's a fun little exercise I do with kids sometimes. I give them a broomstick and tell them to hold it in the palm of their hand. I ask them to focus on the bottom inch of the broomstick in their hand, to stare at it up close, and then to try and balance it. And they can't do it. They get mad. They think it's a trick, especially the boys. But then after I calm them down, I ask them to do the same thing but to stare at the top of the broomstick instead. With almost no effort, they balance the broomstick perfectly. Then I ask them to turn the broomstick sideways and think of it as a timeline. If that bottom inch represents right now, and you only focus on it, then the future has no balance. But when you have your eyes set on future ideas, today usually finds a way to balance itself out. When you set your eyes on something greater, then you do better at today. And you usually enjoy it more too. I know it sounds like a paradox—something that can't possibly be true—but almost anyone who has ever accomplished something great didn't just fall into it. They dreamed it and went after their dreams. So dream and plan. Your day will be brighter, and your future will glow.

When you have your eyes set on future ideas,
today usually finds a way to balance itself out.

Throw Off the Stuff

I stopped watching TV recently. And I only use my computer when I need to. I'm not telling you to do that; I'm just saying I did. It's so easy for teens, actually everyone, to fill their time and space with details. It's as if we fear stillness and silence. And yet almost all of the moments of clarity that I have ever had in life came in still places. I'll tell you about one for me—although it's not exactly something that you stumble into.

I hung out with some monks in Alaska a few times. Not monkeys, monks. The Russian Orthodoxy has a deep heritage in Alaska, and I had made friends with the monks in town. They are so nice and outgoing and funny. And so one day I went out fishing to some far-off island and asked my buddy if he could drop me at a small island where they had a monastery. So I showed up on this cove on an island whose only inhabitants were a bear and some red-bearded Russian guys in black robes. I was glad to see the Russians and not the bear. But they had huge smiles. Just on a whim, I asked if I could stay with them for a few days, and they said of course. I'll admit it was one of the odder things that I have done, but I'm glad I did.

Their goal in life is to weed out all distractions that interfere with God, and they spend their days praying, doing for others, gardening, building, and living in harmony. They are the first to admit that it's not for everyone, but it's a calling they have chosen. So I spent a few days standing up in services with them (for four to eight *hours*), listening to the ancient prayers that they sing, and taking in the great detail of the church they had carved by hand. They didn't use instruments, just their voices. They used incense to heighten their sense of smell when they prayed. And after a time, I felt a calmness I had never experienced before. I went to bed that night in my sleeping bag on the floor and felt my heart beating loudly—and calmly. I closed my eyes and had the most peaceful night of sleep I have ever had. In the daytime, I sat down by the sunny cove and wrote in my journal. I took in the colors and smells and temperatures. The mountains seemed alive, and I felt at peace. Of course, I got tired of only eating salmon and potatoes, but I am so glad I went there.

For me, that tiny experience was a reminder that the stuff we fill our lives with to make us happy rarely does that for very long. If you are bold enough, I highly recommend you toss aside some of the things that distract your time. You might find that by trying something new—or just writing, or walking, or learning to enjoy time to yourself—your happiness can come from strange places. It lasts longer, and it usually costs a whole lot less.

Happiness is not a state to arrive at, but a manner of traveling.

—Margaret Lee Runbeck

Other Happy Secrets That Shouldn't Be Secret

☆ **Have a diverse social life.** Happier people spend less time alone. They consider spending time with friends, loved ones, or family a larger priority than people who are considerably less happy.

☆ **Be healthy.** This doesn't mean being ripped or super slim, but having good health is a huge contributor to feeling healthier and happier. When you take care of your physical self, it will take care of you back. I know that sounds corny, but it's true. So put down the venti-sized-nitrate-laced-sugar-bomb frozen coffee drink already.

☆ **Be open, but not an open book.** Happier young people are open, but they don't tell everything about themselves. There's a balancing act between keeping privacy in your life and being open with the appropriate people. It can be great to have your heart on your sleeve, but it's not always safe there, and it deserves to be protected.

☆ **Avoid lying.** Sounds elementary, but people do it all the time. Lying is a cancer, and it starts patterns that can be detrimental. Just as avalanches start with a few little snowflakes, even the tiniest of lies can snowball on you. So be honest; it's a better way to live life, and you'll sleep better at night. Want people to say "Hi, Liar!"? Me neither.

☆ **Act your age.** If you are fourteen, be fourteen. Don't try to be twenty-one. There is nothing sadder than seeing a twelve-year-old trying to be twenty or thirty (or a forty-year-old trying to be twenty, for that matter). Happier people embrace their age and time in life. Enjoy your youth.

☆ **Be considerate.** Showing respect and being considerate aren't always flashy, but they are seeds that grow deep in people's hearts and root you in good things. When you plant a tree, you won't see how strong it will be for quite some time. But every massive, mighty tree started with a seed. In the same way, strong relationships—with family, with friends, with the opposite sex—begin with the seed of consideration. It's very attractive and will not only make you happier, but you'll also find that being genuinely kind and encouraging can literally change the lives of other people.

Shalom

I realize that happiness is an important thing, but it can also be kind of shallow. I mean, everyone tries to be happy—retailers try to sell it, consumers try to buy it, some people try to kiss it, and some people buy books about how to get it. But if anger is a cover-up feeling for hurt, then happiness is a cover-up emotion for something even deeper.

I have a Jewish friend, and sometimes we laugh about all the words he uses. (He laughed first, so then I knew I could too and wouldn't be called a racist or anything. It would have been awkward if I'd laughed first and he hadn't.) But then I heard him talking to another guy one day, and they looked at one another and had a brief moment of silence after their conversation. The other person was also Jewish. They gave a cordial nod of the head after that moment of silence, and then my friend said one strange, yet calm word to him. I had heard the word plenty of times, and I knew it had something to do with peace, or peace be with you. But something about the way he said it sparked my deeper curiosity. I knew he meant what he had said, but I didn't know what it really meant. So I asked him.

"The word is *shalom*," he said with a smile. And I said, "Oh yeah, that means 'peace' right?" And he said that actually the word had a deeper meaning. He told me that when you say "shalom" to someone, you wish the person peace, no matter what circumstances he or she may encounter. He had wished his friend peace. Not just fun, or happiness, or good luck for the game, but something deeper. And I think that's what we are all looking for anyway. Peace, for all of the great and hard things that we encounter.

So, yes, I wish you happiness, but more than that I also wish for you to find peace. Peace, no matter what your circumstances may be.

I hope you will be someone who is full of shalom.

IT'S NOT OKAY TO BE DUMB

Ever imagine yourself stuck on a remote tropical island? Most people do at some point. What essential things would your island have on it?

Out of all the essentials, my island, I hope, would have coconuts. Coconuts and a book on how to build ships for dummies. And maybe a Marriott. But why the coconuts, you ask? Well, I'm glad you asked. Let me tell you.

The coconut's liquid is some of the most useful on Earth. It has more natural and beneficial sugars and electrolytes than almost any other liquid on the planet, which makes it nature's Gatorade on steroids, if steroids were good. They are not. Coconut liquid also has fatty acids and a bunch of other stuff that helps keep you healthy. And it has the same electrolyte composition as human blood. Because it is sterile, cool, and easily absorbed by the body, it's considered a substitute for blood plasma. It even works as a universal blood donor.

"Sir what is your blood type?"
"Um, I believe that it's coconuts, thank you."

So if you were on an island and had a bad accident, like falling out of a tall tree while gathering coconuts (irony), and you were losing blood and couldn't get to a hospital that had your blood type, coconuts could save your life. Just hook up a coconut IV, or maybe have someone else hook it up since you are bleeding, and now you are still alive instead of dead. Seriously. They actually did this in World War II in the Pacific from 1941 to 1945. Severely wounded American soldiers were given coconut water IVs, and it saved their lives.[1]

P.S. Coconut "milk" is not really milk. There is no such thing as almond milk or soy milk either. News flash: milk comes from animals. Coconuts are not animals. Nor are almonds animals. It is soy, almond, and coconut juice.

I love random factoids of information. My brain breathes them in like oxygen. I'm not saying I would like to get to a point where I am losing enough blood to die. I *am* saying that if this situation stumbled upon me, I would be willing to go with the coconuts just for the story. I mean, come on . . . coconuts!

In other words, there is so much out there to know. Knowledge really seems to be limitless.

I'm so stupid.
I'm so stupid.
I'm so stupid.

This was the thought that resonated in my mind for most of my life growing up. And yet now, if you told me that I was needed to run a shipping business in the Pacific, I would say "Okay, I can do it. I just need some time to learn about the shipping industry, and the Pacific Ocean, and how to run the business, and then I'm in." No biggie, right?

But in high school, sitting in math class and watching people just roll right along with the multiplicative inverse and fractions, then pre-algebra, and algebra, and not to mention history, well, it was awful. The voice inside my head just kept saying, *These kids are smarter than you. They are better than you. That's why they have better clothes, families that are together, girls who like them, better houses, and more money. They know something that you don't, because you stink at everything you do. That's just the way it is. You are stupid, Chad.* And I wasn't even sure why.

When I got expelled from school in the fourth grade for planning a conspiracy to catch my cruel teacher being cruel, I thought, *Why didn't that work? Oh yeah, because I'm stupid. What smart kid gets expelled?* By the sixth grade, I had more than ninety detentions in a year. Why? 'Cause I got annoyed at schoolwork, and I didn't get it, and I was dumb. *Who cares? I'm stupid* was my thinking. I had a permanent seat in detention because it was expected that I would be there. I think I got used to it, you know?

Seventh and eighth grade meant more suspensions, more detentions, bad grades, low attention span. *I must be stupid, of course.* Then other bad decisions came along with the territory. Here's a tip: When someone walks up to you and says, "Hey, I dare you to go punch Adam over there. I hate him," there is a moment when you think that people will think you are strong, or fearless, or not stupid, and different than you have always been. Don't do it! Unfortunately, I did. One day, I walked over to some kid who had never done anything to me. I just looked at him and pulled my shoulder back and punched him right in the face. He fell to the ground, bleeding. The look on his face is hard to forget. He just sat there in pain. I acted like I didn't care, but inside I wanted to cry and say I'm sorry. I wanted to tell him that how he felt at that moment was exactly how I had felt my whole life, and I hated that he was feeling that too. His look of pain and confusion said he didn't understand. Of course, the result was expulsion for fighting again. So once again, it was hard to be accepted at school, because I wasn't there. How did I not see that one coming? *I was stupid, that's why . . .* I had almost forgotten that voice in my head.

If you don't control your mind, someone else will.

—John Allston

When you can't even see the tunnel, much less the light at the end of it, who cares if you stay in that tunnel or just leave? And who cares about stupid sayings with tunnels? And who really cares about love, or youth group stuff, or Bible verses, or doing well in school?

If you put a puppy around a bunch of sheep and raise it as one of the herd, the dog will actually behave like a sheep. It will think it is one. And if you think you are stupid, you will live out that perception of yourself.

If you actually think there is a limit in your life—in who you can be and what you can accomplish—and if you think that limit is small, then you will limit your own life. And guess what? People do it *all* the time.

As a teenager I was so insecure. I was the type of guy that never fit in because he never dared to choose.

I was convinced I had absolutely no talent at all. For nothing. And that thought took away all my ambition too.

—Johnny Depp

Important Factors in Your Life, ◀ Good and Bad

Negative Parents

If you have a parent who tells you how capable and competent you are, especially from a young age, then you will believe it. And you will actually become more capable than someone who doesn't have an encouraging parent. If you have a parent who doesn't tell you how capable you are, well . . . here's what that can sound like.

Hey, Chad,

You always tell us to believe in ourselves, and that's great and all. Thanks for telling us that stuff when you speak. But my problem is that it's hard to believe that when my parents think I'm so dumb. My dad has never told me or my brother anything good about ourselves for our whole life, and it's kinda hard to believe that I'm super special or something great, ya know, when he tells me how I don't know anything, and I'm just a girl, and girls can't do as much as guys, and they don't know anything. He's mean to my mom, and she doesn't ever say anything back, so that's what I have to learn from. I don't really know what I wanna do, and I feel lost a lot of the time. My brother is angry about a lot of stuff, and I know it's because of our parents. I don't have anyone I can talk to about this stuff. I want to believe those things that you told us, but how do I do that when every day I am told how stupid I am? Any advice?

—Monique

Guess what? Some parents are just bad parents. They don't do the things they need to do, like tell their kids how capable they are. I'm not judging them. It's just a fact. Some people are bad at baseball; it happens. And some people are bad at parenting; it happens, and the kids face challenges because of it. I'm sorry if you are someone who hasn't been encouraged by your parents. It can make things harder. But it doesn't have to make things difficult forever.

There are a lot of kids—girls, in particular—who don't have any father figures, or at least not any good ones. That can be hard on both girls and guys, but in different ways. Maybe you haven't had an active dad in your life. Or maybe you have a dad who makes you feel less valuable, or cuts you down, or tells you that you aren't capable of great things. Maybe your mom does some of that stuff too. That is so tough to deal with. I never had a dad who did or said harsh things to me, so I can't really imagine what it would be like to have a parent who makes you feel like "less." But I know it must be really, really difficult.

Just Say No—to Your Parents

Sometimes you can say no to parents. If you have a parent who is making you feel less capable, who is making you feel dumb, who is lowering your self-esteem and your sense of personal dignity, then I say don't listen to them. Seriously. If they tell you to do the dishes, do the dishes. But if they tell you you're dumb, let it go in one ear and out the other. Someday, you will figure out that they are projecting their own feelings of inadequacy onto you, but don't wait to learn that they are not correct. You don't have to listen to other people if they aren't saying things that build you up. Disclaimer: I'm *not* saying to disrespect your parents—if you do something dumb (like drugs or alcohol or harming small animals), they can tell you that you are acting dumb. But I *am* saying you can ignore the thoughtless, hurtful words of parents who disrespect you. You know what I'm talking about.

Dumb Friends

Sometimes it's other kids at school who try to make you feel dumb, less capable, boring, or anything else that keeps you from growing as a person. Maybe they are friends, or acquaintances, or enemies; they come in all shapes, sizes, and flavors, so to speak. Maybe it's the annoying and immature bully who lives to harass people. Maybe it's the naturally talented good-looking kid who just treats you like dirt and is loved by everyone. Maybe it's the guy or the girl who played games with your head and your heart. It's really sad that some kids do this to other kids, but it happens. And when you're in school, you are forced to be around some of these people for eight hours or more a day. The people and the environment of school can help make or break the extent to which you feel smart, capable, able, and excited. It can feel like a prison at times. Speaking of prison . . .

Meanwhile, in Young-People

When I'm sitting in juvenile detention and then in rehab, I am thinking, *This is awful, but so is life.* And I imagine it might have been easy to just ride that slow-moving train to nowhere. It seemed as if a lot of people were on it, and, honestly, they looked pretty comfortable in their seats. Thanks to some people who cared about me and counseled me, I actually got something out of my time there and put some spark in my life . . . and then I had to go back to school. Yippee.

So back to high school, where I had to retake some classes. At that point, I wasn't completely hopeless. I had seen where my life was going, and I decided to try, to start over, and to maybe make some things better in my life. I was even somewhat excited by this whole give-life-a-new-try thing. But I still felt as if the ceiling—rather than the sky—was the limit.

I was optimistic; but I just didn't know what to do with that optimism. So I did what most guys do. I sat quietly in my seat and tried not to look stupid. I really wanted to just blend in. To be . . . ready for it? . . . normal.

Biology class was just not that much fun for me.

Although I liked dissecting frogs, the class itself was just not as much fun as, say, throwing a Frisbee, or eating food, or just breathing in and out. I also had a hard time with math and science in general. But since I was now being quiet in class, I had more of a chance to pay attention. Then, one day, the teacher asked me a question, kind of spur of the moment. You know how some kids really hope the teacher won't randomly call on them to see if they are paying attention? That was me every day of my life. But this time I actually was paying attention. (Mostly because I knew that's what I *should* be doing in class. Being in therapy was correcting some of my behavior, after all.)

The teacher's name—and I kid you not—was Boring. His name was *Mr. Boring*. So one day he called on me, and I simply answered "sulfur oxide." Because I had actually read it in the chapter and remembered it. Then a girl in front of me turned around and said something I had never even thought about myself: "You're really smart, aren't you?"

Life-changing moment.

Wait, what!?! Smart!?! I didn't say a word for the rest of class. Actually, I didn't talk the rest of the day. I just thought about the fact that some person sitting in front of me got the impression that I was intelligent and not stupid. I had never really thought about myself that way. Was I actually smart? Or, more importantly . . .

➤ Is Being Smart a Choice?

Could I decide to be smart? Uh-oh, can you see where I am headed now?

Can someone *decide* to be a smart person?

Yes, he can. It's called being *competent*. And it is a choice. And whether you choose to be competent or incompetent will determine a lot about your life. Competency—believing you are smart and capable of making smart decisions—is kind of an underlying theme to all the subjects in this book. How you see yourself guides a lot of your choices, opinions, and feelings about things like dating, love, friendship, and basically everything else in your life.

Here is a simple example. Suppose I ask you the following question:

A region of India has some pretty bad problems. They are short on drinking water, and there are a lot of waterborne diseases. Conventional wells and water systems haven't worked there. It is affecting trade, education, public health, and the potential for tourism. Money is not an issue. You will have access to all the money you need to fix this problem. Can you figure out a solution?

Now, very simply, will you instinctively say yes or no? Someone who feels competent and capable will likely say, "Yes, I can figure this out. Anything can be figured out with the right effort and with the right people." But if you said no, why is that? Does the problem not interest you? Do you think you couldn't figure it out? Do you feel it's too complicated for you? Maybe you just don't think you can do really big things. Whether you chose to answer yes or no, even though it's a specific question about India, says a lot about how you feel about your potential.

Back to the coconuts for a minute. I know it's random information. My friends tease me and call me the random guy. "Hey, Chad, tell us a random fact that has to do with volcanoes. Oh wait, and one about the history of running." When I start a sentence with "Did you know that . . . ," my good friends usually respond with, "I mean, why wouldn't you know that a violin contains about seventy different types of wood? That's common sense, right?" Or, "Of course the Rx symbol on a prescription bottle stands for the astrological sign for Jupiter." And you know what I don't do after that? Apologize. I don't apologize for the fact that I like facts. I don't apologize for my desire to learn about anything and everything, and places, and people, and science, and writing, and history, and quirky traditions of Amazonian tribes. I don't think I'm exceptionally smart at all. It's just that I seriously love to learn. It's part of who I am now. And people appreciate that, as long I keep it under control. I realized it that day in biology class—in Mr. Boring's class of all places, I know. When class ended that day, I made a life-changing decision. At the time I didn't really think it was that big of a decision, but it was. At third period, on a Wednesday, I decided that I was going to be a capable person. I decided that I could learn things. I told myself that I was smart. And guess what? I am smart. I am competent. And I realize now that it is a choice.

How you see yourself guides a lot of your choices, opinions, and feelings about things like dating, love, friendship, and basically everything else in your life.

And that's how I know that you are smart. You are a competent and capable human being—if you choose to be.

What Is Competence, Anyway?

Do you know what *competence* means? Maybe the biological definition will help explain. Biologically speaking, when a cell is competent, it means that the cell has the ability to take up extracellular or "naked" DNA from its environment. In other words, it can absorb the information surrounding it.[2]

Being competent is the ability to take in the information around you.

Competency Paints a More Accurate Picture

High school and low self-esteem. Often related. But you should know that one of the many benefits of choosing competency is that it usually paints a more accurate picture of yourself. Being competent is also a pretty great jumping-off point for healthy self-esteem. People with a high sense of competency and good self-esteem actually have a more accurate perception of themselves. People with a low self-esteem usually have inaccurate, and even over-inflated, views of their capability. I mean, *"I'm awesome at everything"* is a somewhat suspect statement. People who say that either don't really believe it or have an inaccurate view of themselves. Teens with a higher sense of competency see their abilities and accomplishments more accurately. *"I don't do that well with math, but I'm great at writing and the social aspects of journalism, so I plan to go to school for that"* is something that a competent person could say confidently. And that person wouldn't sound conceited, just certain of things and able to feel good about them. I like people who know themselves well. It's kind of refreshing.

*You are a competent and capable
human being—if you choose to be.*

You Are Strong *and* Wimpy

Do you know what some of your strengths are? Your weaknesses? It's a good idea to write these sorts of things down. Writing them down makes them more measurable.

Here are a few of the things that I know I'm good at:

∞ **I love to learn.** I can take a lot of information and simplify it in ways that others enjoy.

∞ **I give good advice.** I can listen and supply input to help people make their own decisions while also telling them what I think about something.

∞ **I'm responsible.** People trust me, and I am a dependable person. If I say I will do it, then I will do it.

∞ **I make other people feel comfortable.** I'm not an incredible ice-breaker, but I make people feel relaxed and connected in a crowd of strangers.

∞ **I'm pretty decent with humor.** In writing (sometimes), making fun of myself, or lightening up situations. And I enjoy making other people laugh.

How about you? What are some things you are good at?

_____

_____

_____

_____

_____

Things I'm horrible at (at least sometimes):

∞ **Patience.** I have it to a point, and then I hit a wall and lose my patience. I need more of it, and I need to work on becoming more patient. That includes keeping my mouth shut when I lose my patience.

∞ **Being optimistic.** Although I can be optimistic, I can tend toward pessimism and being negative if I don't watch myself. It's easy for me to point out the flaws in something before I see what is right. This can offend people if I'm not careful.

∞ **Confusing facial expressions.** My body language and facial expressions can often be the opposite of what I am thinking inside. Makes for awkward situations sometimes.

∞ **Consistency.** I prefer to change pace after a while

with work and subject materials. I am consistent in personality; but when it comes to work, I get bored quickly, and this can be a problem.

∞ **Works well with others—kind of.** I love being part of a team, but I have to be careful. Sometimes hearing people tell me that they like what I talk about, or that they love reading my books, gives me an over-inflated sense of self if I take it in the wrong way. It can give me a sense of "entitlement" to my opinions that I have to be humble with, or else I'll just become a large tool bag.

How about you? What are some things that you are not so good at?

_____

_____

_____

_____

_____

_____

Everyone has their own strengths and weaknesses. And knowing them helps you honestly evaluate yourself and keep your self-esteem in balance. It also helps you understand yourself and your friends more. It makes you more aware. That is a good thing, and competent human beings are aware.

The Problem with Smart People

There is a story that fascinates me. Malcolm Gladwell is an author who writes books with peculiar scenarios. Needless to say, I like him. And the information applies here. It also has to do with really smart people, who aren't much different from you.

In a book called *Outliers*, which looks at people who are super unique, Gladwell asks, "Why?" Is there really a contributing single factor that makes Bill Gates, Hannah Montana, and Steve Jobs the people they are? Is there anything that makes people successful beyond just their capabilities? Meaning, are they really that exceptionally unique or smart or talented? It turns out . . . not really. Most of the time anyway. They just happened to be in the right place, or in the right place during the right period in history, or they learned how to get what they want from the world.

Take Chris Langan, for example. Some people consider him to be one of the smartest people alive. His IQ can't accurately be measured because he tests off the charts. He spoke at six months old. When he was five, he started questioning people about the existence of God but wasn't pleased with the lack of answers he got. He was *five*! In school, he could walk into a foreign language class, skim the textbook in three to five minutes, and then ace any foreign language test, never having known a word of it. When he was a teenager, working as a farmhand, he started to read and work on theoretical physics. He got a perfect score on his SAT, even though he never studied and fell asleep during the test. Without guitar lessons, he could play note for note some of the most difficult songs of some of the most talented musicians. He would casually make drawings that people thought were actual photographs, even though he had had no art lessons. And that's just the start.

Chris's mind is able to see questions and answer them as though they are simple puzzles. But here is the problem. Even though Chris is considered to be a genius, it would seem he has missed out on some things in life, especially for someone with his natural potential. He could be working in the best universities in the world, continuing his paper on how the universe works using a new model of physics that he has been working on. But he had to leave college because his mom messed up his financial papers. He failed physics class, even though he knew more than the professor, because he was hitchhiking fifteen miles a day in the snow to get to class and missed the test. He wasn't able to communicate that to his professor, who might have been more understanding. I mean, who would even be willing to put in that much effort just to get to school? But instead he worked on a clam boat, in factory jobs, and as a bouncer at a bar. Since Gladwell included the story about Chris in his book, Chris has received a lot more opportunity and recognition for his unique abilities.

He continues to write something called the "Cognitive-Theoretic Model of the Universe," and does this from a horse farm in Missouri, where he now lives. There is no doubt he is a genius with a one-in-a-billion mind. It's also great that he is now being taken a lot more seriously. The sad part is it seems that he missed out on a lot early in life because he didn't express himself.

And what about you and me? We might not ace the SAT exams while falling asleep, but we are reasonably smart people. And yet reasonably smart people can succeed or fail at things in life for the exact same reasons that Chris seemed to struggle. And here is why:

The Magic Answer

The ability to express yourself. That's it. The magic answer. The thing that seems to have so much power in determining success in life, relationships, school, and careers. Communication is how we navigate through this world. It's one of the keys to feeling capable and competent. Being able to express yourself allows you to interact with the world and the people in it. Communication allows you to defend yourself, to assert yourself, and to declare who you are and what you know. By interacting with the world and its people, it allows you to realize your capability and to influence the world around you so that you can succeed in it.

But Chris Langan was never taught or encouraged to express himself. Instead, his stepfather barked commands at him. He wasn't nurtured in the things that he did well. He wasn't encouraged to argue, to debate, or to learn to give his opinions and ask questions. People talked to him, and he thought a lot, but he never learned how to talk back. He just accepted whatever he was handed for his life.[3]

But you need to realize that you can shape the world around you; you can choose to be capable. It sounds simple. Almost too simple. But it is true.

Maybe you don't realize that you are smart, capable, and competent. Or maybe you don't see how being competent relates to dating, which is why you're reading this book in the first place. But it does. When you see yourself as a smart, capable, competent person, it will help your dating relationships, your marriage, your friendships.

Or maybe you don't see how being competent relates to dating, which is why you're reading this book in the first place. But it does.

Decide for Yourself

Stop and think for a moment about the things and people in your life and how they affect the way you feel about yourself. Maybe it's the people at your school. Maybe it's the social hog who talks over you and everyone else. Maybe it's your parents or siblings and the way they treat you. They probably don't mean to make you feel dumb or incompetent. Most of the time people don't even know that they are doing it to others. But it happens. And when it does, don't be like some trained animal. Don't just sit back and take it. Decide for yourself that you have a voice, that you can express what you think and what you need. Decide to be competent.

Lies You May Encounter on the
Road to Being Competent

Competent Isn't "In"

I know the terms "cool, "in," and "popular" really aren't used that much anymore. But guess what? The behaviors are still there. Here is why. . . .

Chad,

I'm struggling with the whole identity thing at my school. I know you have talked before about respecting myself and not being afraid of who I am, but it seems like the girls who just act dumb and clueless attract a lot of guys. No one wants to be with the smart girl who loves to read and likes history. I dunno. Just seems depressing that people at my school don't like smart. What do you think?

—Mandy

Well, Mandy, it is kind of a bummer when certain people and schools don't seem to value being smart, but it's not that way everywhere. And there are a whole lot of people who love history and reading. Use your smarts to find other people like yourself—people who enjoy learning. Simply put, don't buy the lie. You'll want to return your purchase later. I mean, do you really want to be with a guy who is only interested in girls who act dumb?

Chad,

Hey, I'm Mark. Since you and I talked a few months ago, I've been thinking about how you said girls really appreciate a smart and confident and kind guy. I try to be that. I mean, I have a lot to learn, but I am smart, and I'm not trying to be the football hero or the cool guy. It just doesn't seem to go over well. Girls get obsessed with guys' looks too and how they act like the awesome cocky guy. It feels like it's the other way around. What would you say to guys like me?

—Mark, but I already told you that

It really does go both ways. And the answers look an awful lot alike too. See, we have plenty in common with each other.

And one more thing to remember: high school isn't forever. When it comes to colleges, careers, and the whole rest of your life in general, it's the smart kids people are looking for.

I Can't Do Anything Incredible

Doing remarkable things isn't limited to losing both arms and legs, going blind, and still overcoming the odds to win the gold medal in the Olympics for downhill slalom racing. "I'm just ordinary" is a thought that has kept people down for centuries. And oddly enough, some of the most monumental achievements in history are done by ordinary people. Those people just realized that they were capable. And so are you. Choose your adventure. Find something you get excited about, and then find out what the world needs. You'll do amazing things you can't even imagine.

I can do everything by the power of Christ. He gives me strength.

—Philippians 4:13 NIV

Stuff that Steals Your Time

One of the best ways to keep people from reaching their potential is to distract them. I mean, it's pretty simple—and effective. I'm not really going to come down on Facebook or TV or the blah-blah-blah cheesy stuff you'd expect to hear. But it is important to not be distracted by things that simply occupy your time and don't contribute anything real to your life. Here are some things that work really well in the art of distraction:

∞ boyfriends

∞ girlfriends

∞ drama (and you know what I mean!)

∞ social networking sites, the Internet, and your *unbelievable* amount of texts

∞ TV

∞ video games

These probably aren't a surprise to you, but these things do surprisingly well at keeping people from developing their own unique tastes, joys, hobbies, and individual strengths. Your time is valuable. Make sure it isn't stolen from you.

Competency Isn't that Important

I mean, I'm the one who decided to tell you that competency *is* valuable. So is it really? Some people might not think so. Maybe it's just a made-up term that I'm pushing on you to make you think.

Well, maybe I am pushing it. But it's because competency is about your character. And the later in life that people start thinking about it, the more they have to play catch up. The sooner you start focusing on your abilities, your capabilities, your strengths, and your potential, the more you are steering a course that will land you in a great spot. It will help you when you date, it will help you in deciding what you want to study, and it will help you in the self-worth department. It's never too early to start declaring your capability, and then investing in it. Sorry, I sound like a dad there. Now eat your vegetables.

Stealing Your Soul and Selling It Back

This section may seem like it has nothing whatsoever to do with dating. But it actually does. There are people out there who don't care a thing about you. People who will take every bit of who you are for a dollar and never think twice about you. They surround your life, and they are *in* your life every day. They are in your shoes, your notebook, the songs you listen to, the food you eat, the way you think relationships work, and where you go for fun. They try to steal your ability to make your own decisions by playing off the fears, insecurities, and desires that all teenagers have—especially when it comes to your relationships with the opposite sex. And I can't in good conscience believe that being naïve to the world they try to create will do you any good.

Who are these seemingly bad humans? Who are these people who are out to steal your wallet, your identity, and your uniqueness by changing you and every other teenager into the person they tell you to be? Marketing machines.

As a teenager, your body is going crazy. It's an easy thing to exploit. Simply take a personal desire—popularity, good looks, sexuality, stylishness, power—and turn it into a product. *Wear our perfume or cologne to make your date go nuts. Buy our shoes—they give you an instant skater California look. Use this hair wax and the girl at the beach will love you instantly.* Promise to give someone what he or she desires, put a price tag on it, and watch that desire come pouring into the bank. It's what these people do all the time. But all that stuff that promises to reveal the *real* you just makes you look like everyone else. It makes you a clone.

This is the time to be competent, to use your prefrontal cortex. It's your money (actually, it's usually your parents' money), it's your identity, and those are your hopes and desires and fears. Your identity is unique. You are not a clone, and I hope you won't ever let yourself be.

When it comes to being competent and capable, the good news is that you have the choice. You can choose to turn on your brain. You can choose to exercise your mind, to reason, to think, and *to think for yourself.* The computer won't do it for you. Clever sayings and sleek clothing brands won't do it for you. Other people won't do it for you either. It's your choice. You have to make it.

You are a competent, capable human being. More so than you know. Everyone can be, if they choose to be. You don't have to be a genius. You just need to know you are valuable. You are worth it. You are highly thought of. God knows how capable, smart, and competent you can be. He gave you that brain and heart for a reason. He wants you to treat them like a muscle, with a lot of care and plenty of exercise.

12

THE PROBLEM WITH FALLING IN LOVE WITH MYTHICAL CREATURES

That Can Bite You or Possibly Ruin Your Life

How much do you sleep? Five hours? Ten hours?

Sleep is a strange thing, and, to be honest, doctors don't completely understand its purpose or why some people need more or less of it than others. Sleep is thought to be vital for repairing the muscles and tissues of the body, as well as the nervous and immune systems. And if you go too long without sleep, you can experience exhaustion, sickness, hallucinations, and eventually death.

Although there are some cultures where only a few hours of sleep are sufficient—such the Piraha tribe of the Amazon, for whom only a short siesta serves as the way to sleep—no one can go too long without any sleep. Well, almost no one.

Meet Ngoc Thai. He hasn't slept since 1973. That's thirty-seven years without sleep, shattering the record of eleven days set by a magician in 1964. Ngoc is a Vietnamese farmer who came down with a fever one day in 1973. Since the fever broke, he has been unable to sleep. He is now in his sixties and says that a lack of sleep does not affect him physically. He still carries two 110-pound sacks of rice more than two miles every day to his house. He has tried everything in order to sleep, but medications and folk remedies have never worked, and doctors don't have a good explanation. To this day, Ngoc has gone more than twelve thousand nights without sleeping.[1]

In other words, except for a unique Vietnamese farmer named Ngoc, nighttime and sleep are important. Unless, of course, you are a mythical creature.

▶▶ Tastes Like Boogers? Really? Who Tested That?

There are things that look real, and then we find out that they are not. I ate a grass-flavored Harry Potter jelly bean once, and you know what? It tasted a whole lot like grass. It was like a magic trick being played on my taste buds. If you've had them, you know what I'm talking about. For the record, I've never actually eaten a booger, and I'm proud of that, but the booger jelly bean had me pretty convinced that I now know what they taste like.

People have believed a lot of strange things throughout history. They have believed that people who sneezed were witches. They thought the earth was flat for a long time. Even today we believe strange things, like if we have a great car, a cute boyfriend or girlfriend, and great friends, then life will be good. And a lot of us believe if we have love given to us, then we will be content and complete. And while these are appealing wishes to believe in, we should be smarter than that.

There are things that look real, and then we find out that they are not.

Hairy Creatures and Love ◄

I have always been fascinated by some of the stories we all grew up with. I remember being forced to watch *Beauty and the Beast* once—and *only* once. Besides not being the biggest Disney fan (sorry), I was also confused by a few things when I saw that story. Most people saw it as a love story, but I couldn't help but notice that it was essentially a story about an angry, abusive guy/beast who was lost, violent, and hurting. Belle comes along and sees his "magical heart" within. She loves him just because, even though he is mean and violent. Maybe it's because she sees glimpses of gentleness and pain. She wants to love and rescue him. He doesn't really do that many good things for her; she just sacrifices herself out of love for him and then—*poof!*—he miraculously becomes a prince. Not to rain on your parade, and sorry if you like the movie (I'm sure the dancing plates and forks are cute), but that is an incredibly dangerous version of love.

But that story plays itself out all the time in real life, whether the "beast" is a guy or a girl. And you know what? It isn't a Disney movie. And they don't dance happily ever after in the end. Usually people get hurt, and hearts get damaged.

Vampires, Werewolves, and Zombies— You're Still Here?

I'm not going to try and demonize vampires—although I think technically in folklore, they are considered demons. I don't really care to launch some huge rally against werewolves or vampires or any other mythical creatures that teens seem to fall in love with lately. Although zombies never really catch on in the love department. Maybe it's because they can't really talk, and girls like to talk. Also, they have body parts falling off, and they smell even worse than Axe body spray because they are rotting. Anyhoo . . . these are fads, and they will soon disappear, although not soon enough for me and a lot of people I know. But there are some truths that go deeper than the fads that we can learn from, and they will last longer than any book or movie.

Dumbest vampire joke I could find:

Q: Who is a vampire likely to fall in love with?

A: The girl necks door.

First, let's face some facts: Vampires have terribly unhealthy skin. They are skinny and have no blood flow in their lips. And, like it or not, people are attracted to good skin tone; it makes you look healthier and happier. So people who have no blood in their un-rosy cheeks are not going to seem as happy. And guess who doesn't want to sit around with Sad Sally or Sam? Most people, actually. When given the opportunity, most people prefer to hang out with people who are enjoyable to be around.

As for werewolves, they smell bad. My neighbor's dog takes a walk for fifteen minutes, and the smell makes me want to take a shower. And it's a sweet dog. Well, actually, the dog I was talking about jumped out of the window and passed away (rest in doggie heaven, Jasper), but the new dog pretty much smells the same. Werewolves salivate a lot too, and they run around on all fours. Sure, they are strong, but they always seem to be running around in the woods eating weird stuff, howling, going nuts when the moon is full. And there are a lot of social events that you would miss out on, like movies and dances and prom. The werewolves would probably want to stay in the woods where they could sniff all the other werewolves' butts and growl and drool. I mean, maybe it would be exhilarating for a weekend or two for the outdoor enthusiasts, but seriously, all the time? There is more to life than full moons, after all.

Can you imagine a real date with one of these creatures?

Bad Teeth Date Night

VAMPIRE BRO (VAMPS): Go out with me. I must have you for myself.

SALLY: Ummm . . . you talk old-fashioned, and that's a little forward, but you seem confident. I like that. I guess I could go out with you. Wait. What did you mean "for yourself"? You've got a little dried-up, red stuff next to that snaggletooth, by the way.

VAMPS: I shall have you. I must have you. You must come to me in secret. I sleep during the day, so we will have to hang out in the middle of the night. And no friends or parents; they don't understand me, and they probably won't like what I drink . . . I mean, eat.

SALLY: Um . . . okay. Kind of weird. But I want to hang out with you. Besides your bad complexion, there is pain in your eyes, and I sense a deeper longing in your heart that makes me curious. I've always had a weak spot for bad boys. I could see you turning into a great guy. I guess I'll have to sneak out since you aren't interested in the day very much. Too bad. The weather has been really nice, but I don't want you to burn out your retinas from taking a leisurely walk. What are we going to do?

VAMPS: We will sit and be very intense. I will be dark and mysterious. I don't know any jokes, and I'm not into laughing. I might chuckle, but I won't like it. I'm way into seriousness and feeling the dark weight of the world on my soul and all of the things I have seen for centuries. I'm probably going to be emotionally distant and then all of a sudden really emotionally intense. It will probably excite you at first, but then it's going to create a lot of anxiety for you. I also have some pretty serious control issues. So after this date I'm going to make sure that I distance you from your friends and your family. I'll want you to devote your whole heart and self to me. We will be forbidden to be together, so that might cause some problems. But don't worry; I'll tell you over and over that I want to be with you.

SALLY: Umm, I'm having some doubts. I was looking forward to getting to know you. But this is really going to mess with my homework and the spring break plans that I had with my best friend. I like going to the beach.

VAMPS: I also have strong urges to bite people. So maybe wear a turtleneck. I could freak out and scar up your neck pretty good. And one other thing: if we kiss, I might make your heart stop . . . literally. Just a heads-up. Ready to hang?

SALLY: You know what? I'm seeing some red flags here.

The reason that this whole vampire/werewolf fad interests me is because there is a much deeper message that exists in it—and one that will affect people long after Edward, the werewolves, or whatever other mythical creature with bad teeth vanishes into the past.

These stories and fantasies sell us ideas about love. If they were just stories, that would be one thing. But people take that longing, romance, and infatuation, and they create fantasies that play themselves out in people's lives. Even if they don't realize it. In fact, a lot of the messages that we are constantly fed about relationships can actually destroy them. I don't want that to happen to you.

A Bestseller in Three Easy Steps

So here is the simple formula for creating a fantasy . . . and why it usually appeals to girls.

Step 1: The Empty Shell

First, create a main character who is basically an empty shell. This is usually the girl in the story. Note little about her appearance, so that the reader can easily slip herself into the character's place and fantasize about being her.

Usually the heroine is confused, lost, and struggling. She is likely to be awkward and insecure. She is sad because her life is hard. Deep down, she just wants to be rescued and understood. This is something most teens can relate to. It's an awkward time, but odds are, you know that already.

Once the reader relates to the common struggles of this main character—family situation, being misunderstood, hating high school, being bad at sports, or bad luck with guys—she begins to bond to this character. In essence, she becomes her. Now, if only the perfect person would come along to rescue her.

Step 2: Introduce the Second Character

This second character will be the perfect, idealized man. He is what every woman longs for, or so they think. Next, exaggerate all the details about him. His appearance will be striking. His face, his perfect body, his piercing eyes that see into his love's heart, his smell, and even his breath.

Not only is he physically everything a girl would desire, but he is an incredible listener. He wants to hear everything in her heart, and he understands perfectly. He only cares about her, even though she has done nothing to earn this devotion. He is a centuries-old immortal, and he just really wants to date a high school chick with issues. This sounds reasonable, right?

This creates the perfect male, who can then be worshipped by the imaginative reader. I mean, who wouldn't want someone who longs only for them? By this point, all of the crazy behavior—watching someone while she sleeps or forbidding her from being around anyone else—will start to look like love. But in reality, it's super creepy, and it's called *stalking*. And in the real world, parents don't appreciate peeping toms or Edwards.

Step 3: Details Don't Really Matter

After the two main characters are established, the details don't really matter. The reader is hooked into an idealized fantasy and projects it onto an imaginary figure. Together they brush away society and live for one another. Their only happiness is in one another. Nothing exists outside of their love, and that love becomes the goal at any cost.[2]

The problem? Without really realizing it, those idealized and unrealistic ideas about love become part of the reader's heart and head. And those fantasies get projected onto real people.

Oh, Hi, Reality

In reality—you know, the real world we actually live in—the male character—like a popular vampire, for example—is a high school nightmare. He doesn't do anything, but all the girls like him. He is probably insecure and overcompensates with a cocky, arrogant attitude. His actions are completely selfish. He thinks about only what he needs, even if he thinks he needs someone else's love to satisfy him.

He is controlling and does not value the people around him, because to value people means to sacrifice for them. And he has no interest in doing that. What is presented as perfection and love in a novel or a movie is neither perfection nor anything close to love. It is emotionally abusive and oppressive, and it keeps people from growing.

Oh Yeah, and for the Guys

It works the other way around for guys. We are sold all kinds of lies about relationships. Since guys don't read nearly as many novels, or hardly any books, we take to magazines. Whether it's dirt-bike magazines, skating, or workout and fitness stuff, they are littered with relationship advice that we don't even realize we are being hit with.

Guys don't seem to have the same obsession with mythical creatures. I think we are more okay with the way girls look and act in the real world. Guys might idealize girls physically, but they seldom turn them into strange beasts that run around in the night. So congrats on not having to be mythical creatures to grab our interest . . . in a weird way, I guess.

But guys are repeatedly told one simple thing: all we need are buddies, freedom, and good-looking girls who want us, and we'll be the happiest guys on Earth. The lie that guys get sold involves bodies, money, sex, and beauty—and no self-sacrifice or commitment on our part.

Well, I will tell you something. I know guys who have this. I know them personally. Great-looking, wealthy, independent, world travelers, business owners, famous, and well-respected. And in almost every case, they are miserable. The lie they are buying does not satisfy them. It's intoxicating, and it seems to offer everything. But in reality, it steals everything that brings real satisfaction. The guys I know who date and have sex with multitudes of women are the unhappiest and the most insecure. They are trying to find value while denying the value in everything around them.

Most of the things I have talked about in this chapter are the opposite of anything good in relationships. Healthy relationships involve two people who nurture one another, give hope, listen, care, and ask for care in return. They grow. They bring joy and peace. They heighten your dreams and scope of the world, and they inspire you to move mountains.

You are free to make your own choices. But make them well. You deserve care, and the people around you do too. And you deserve to make decisions that will serve your heart and the hearts around you well.

So keep your neck covered. Play with the dogs; don't date them. I think it just works better that way.

13

WHY THIS BOOK COULD BE STUPID

How many seconds are in the memory span of a goldfish? I was always told around five seconds. As it turns out, it's way more than three or five seconds, or even a minute. It's at least three months. It has also been proven beyond reasonable doubt that a goldfish can remember and tell the difference in colors, sounds, and shapes. It can also learn to push a small lever in order to get a food reward. Even if the lever only worked for about an hour each day, the goldfish can learn to push the lever only during the hour that it dispenses food. It will leave it alone the other twenty-three hours of the day. We know this because it's been proven by the department of psychology at the University of Plymouth.[1]

(How do I get into *that* program? Probably would have been more fun than calculus.) In other words, goldfish are not as simple as we have been led to believe. And people aren't either. You are one of these people.

Although I hope you don't think that the book is completely stupid (I put a lot of time and heart into it, thank you), I do hope that people will consider that one book trying to define complex things in life, completely and for everyone, would be a stupid and unrealistic promise. But allow me to try another route in making my point, which involves a somewhat promiscuous (and entirely fictional) woman of the seventeenth century.

▶ The Clothing of Promiscuous Women a Couple Hundred Years Ago

Once upon a time, there was a girl who wore a scarlet letter on her chest. It didn't say Hollister, or Gap, or anything like that, but you probably already guessed that. Back then it was a bad thing to have a letter sewn onto your outfit. In this particular story, it was a sign that everyone was calling you a . . . well . . . a little loose. It's true, sorry. Regardless of rigorously conservative and even odd Puritan traditions, the whole scarlet letter thing was mean even for them. Geez. Even mean teenagers aren't always mean, twenty-four hours a day, forever.

Side note: When did it become *not* strange to wear brand names on our chests? Am I on crazy pills, or does this seem backward? Really. "Sure, I'll be your billboard, random clothing company that charged me too much for this sweatshirt with the name in oversized font. And no, don't pay me. I'll pay you!" (The author apologizes for this late-night, coffee-induced outburst.)

You might have guessed that I'm talking about the story of *The Scarlet Letter*. At some point in your high school experience, you may be forced to read it. But it's a great story, and I hope that you don't hate it just because your English teacher tries to force you to appreciate great historical literature while owning too many cats. Or was that just mine? It seems like the equivalent of making a kid appreciate vegetables by forcing them down the kid's throat. "See? Aren't they delicious? Vegetables are good for you. You see?" Aaahhh! So if you're forced to read *The Scarlet Letter*, you might not like it as much and not see the great writing and deeper story underneath. Forced reading is probably why people run to cheat off CliffsNotes. Or ... maybe you've already read it and you liked it. Then ... good for you, and ... um ... forget those last few sentences.

The Scarlet Letter, which was written in 1850 by Nathaniel Hawthorne, is a story about Hester Prynne and is set in Boston during the seventeenth century. I know how much this information excites you. It gets better though. The story starts out as a young woman with an infant is being taken from prison and brought to the middle of town. She has a "rag of scarlet cloth" on the breast of her gown in the shape of the letter *A*, which is assumed to stand for *adultery*. Here's the great part. She has a baby and is being brought to the town square so that everyone can taunt her and help make her feel really terrible. You know, in case giving birth in prison was too much fun. Awesome, huh? Hester's husband did not travel to the United States with her, and he was later presumed to have been lost at sea on his way to meet her. So it seems Hester had an affair while in Boston and got pregnant. Now her baby is her shame, but she won't tell who the father is.

Now, this is back when being a Puritan was bigger and more important than being a Boston Celtics or Red Sox fan. There wasn't really a separation of church and state, so, basically, you needed to be a Puritan in order to be a part of society. The people were accustomed to all the Puritan rituals and rules and traditions, not to mention the nifty sport coats and those stylish straight pants and boring shoes. There weren't really a lot of options to choose from in Puritan life, and this included ways to live life, forgive, love, and move on from the past.

The basic—the *very* basic—story is this (and I apologize in advance for the story spoiler): The highly respected minister of the town, Arthur Dimmesdale, is actually the father of Hester's baby. She has to publicly announce her shame and her sin by wearing the letter *A* on her chest. Dimmesdale chooses not to confess his mistake publicly but instead keeps it a secret. But his secret eats at him until it eventually makes him physically sick and almost drives him mad. Hester is forced to the outskirts of town and has to live in a little cottage. She is considered a dirty stain upon society, and the townspeople want nothing to do with her or her "sin child," Pearl.

Here is where the story gets interesting. Hester, instead of choosing to live in the shame of her mistake, consciously decides to live a life of quiet dignity. She fills her days with charitable deeds and humility. Eventually, Hester's character overcomes much of the hatred targeted at her, and she almost wins the respect of people. Now, there's a whole other part of the book about how her husband actually isn't dead, and how he takes on a different name and tries to figure out who she had the affair with so he can punish the man. But I won't bore you with all those details here, because I'm really focusing on Hester and her choices and not the other characters.

So Hester and Dimmesdale eventually decide to run away to Europe and live the rest of their lives with one another and their daughter, who has not known that the minister was really her dad. I'm not endorsing this, by the way; it's just part of the story. Don't yell at me.

In the end, Dimmesdale finally confesses to the community that he is the father. Unfortunately, right after he makes the speech, he drops dead, and you're like "What just happened?!?" So just Hester and Pearl leave Boston. And then some other stuff happens, but it's kind of outside the scope of what intrigued me. And really, the main point of the story in the first place really revolves around the ideas of sin, conformity, humanity, secrets, forgiveness . . . you know . . . all that serious stuff.

Mistakes, Mess-Ups, and Other Stuff Like That

The reason this story is so interesting to me, and hopefully to you, is because there are two things that really pertain to life today. Your life, in particular. The first is sin. Sin is a profound theme throughout this story. Sin is considered a wrongdoing. It means "to fall short" of God's ideals and desires for your life. And sin, mistakes, regrets, and shortcomings are a theme in everyone's life in some way.

The second thing that sticks out to me in this story is how people choose to deal with the mistakes in their lives. Do they choose to hide their life's shortcomings and live in secret shame? Or do they choose to be open about their mistakes, deal with them, and move on? You're going to make mistakes. It's a part of being human. The key is to learn from them. Hold your head high and live a life of dignity. Don't let your past mistakes dictate your life.

> All men make mistakes, but only wise men learn from their mistakes.
>
> —Winston Churchill

One of the saddest things that I see young people do is drown in their mistakes. It happens all the time, and it happened to me as well. I share earlier in the book that I was locked up in a long-term rehab when I was a teenager. I spent almost two years in either rehab, juvenile detention, or outpatient therapy. To over-simplify it, I wasn't happy; I was miserable. Which is why it's important to talk about how *not* to be miserable. (You know, like in chapter 9.) Everything in my life felt miserable. I felt stupid, lonely, insecure, lost, and confused. And I made poor choices in just about everything. I didn't have a lot of guidance, and so I just kind of followed the first flashy things that I saw. Which, of course, were bad decisions, girls, drugs, and so forth. Not good. Then, before you know it, I was sitting in a locked, padded room with other messed-up kids who had raped people, done other unspeakable acts, or just jumped in the same boat that I was in and were stranded on the Island of the Lost and Confused.

I sat in that place for over three months, just cussing at people and refusing to accept that I had problems. And some of the other kids did the same thing. But there were others who came clean. They started talking about their feelings and the things that had happened in their lives to get them there. They genuinely wanted to stop feeling miserable.

Here's the reality: The people who didn't want to be miserable anymore, and who chose not to be miserable, were the ones who did better. The people who wallowed in their misery continued to experience the misery they had had. And they also found new misery everywhere they looked to add to their misery collection. I know this seems like I'm making it all black and white, but when it comes down to it, it is.

Once I decided that I had had enough of the anger and self-loathing, I simply made a decision to change. I'm not giving myself credit. I just didn't want to be unhappy anymore. I was tired of it. I hated it. Being miserable didn't feel good. As odd as that sounds, I realized I wanted to be happy, or at least not miserable.

Most people are more comfortable with old problems than with new solutions.

—Unknown

Big moments in life seem to always start with those little moments of decision. But it first takes a decision. And then it takes putting that decision into action, which can take time. But the first step is the decision.

Big moments in life seem to always start with those little moments of decision.

The idea of Boston with a bunch of Puritans a few hundred years ago seems like a great, rad, fun time. Or not. It sounds pretty awful, actually. The Puritans aren't the reason I like *The Scarlet Letter*. I mean, just the whole "dressing up" all the time thing would drive me crazy. Do I really need to wear a suit to dinner or to walk through the town square? No, I don't. I need my rainbow sandals, shorts, and a T-shirt. Then some Puritan-type would probably call me the devil and hang me or burn me at the stake. So needless to say, I wouldn't love the vibe of the town. Just my guess. Go Red Sox.

I like *The Scarlet Letter* because Hester holds her head high, even in the midst of the shame that the townspeople are trying to heap on her. This I like greatly. Even though Hester must wear the scarlet *A* on the outside, she doesn't wear her guilt on the inside. She moves forward with her life with a dignity that cannot be taken away. This is what her character conveys: choosing dignity in an undignified situation. Hester walks a path of her own choosing, instead of walking along the one that has been chosen for her by other people and by her own past mistakes. I like that. After all, who doesn't relate to hard struggles at some point in life?

> The conventional view serves to protect us from the painful job of thinking.
>
> —J. K. Galbraith

After . . . Is What Matters

I get letters and e-mails all the time. They usually go something like this:

Hey Chad,

    I slept with my boyfriend.

    I lied to my friend.

    I stole from my job.

    I have let guys disrespect me my whole life.

    I have never been told I was valuable, and I don't

        like myself.

    I don't think anyone will ever like me or love me.

    I don't know anything about myself.

    I struggle with believing in God.

    I don't want to share my faith.

    I keep trying to find my value in the people I date.

    I can't stand my parents and the way they treat me.

    I was mean to my friend in front of other people.

    I use girls to make myself feel better.

    I make fun of people but I feel bad inside.

The list goes on and on and on. Teenagers—and people of all ages—do things that are bad. That's no huge surprise. It's what they do *after* the bad things that interests me.

Successful people, owners of companies, new idea makers, world changers, innovative thinkers—they are often the people who encounter the most obstacles. Maybe they have their own shortcomings, or maybe they encounter the world's shortcomings. But successful people become successful not by avoiding failure, but by learning from it. They embrace life's lessons and live better because of it.

It is better to fail in originality than to succeed in imitation.

—Herman Melville

So why do I hope that you will find this book at least a little bit stupid? Because it's *my* opinion. Who I am to tell you how to live your life? I'm one person. I know a few things about a few things, and maybe that information is helpful. But *you* have to decide that. Don't just take me at my word. Take what I have to say and think about it. Really *think* about it. And pray about it too. You can agree or disagree—it's your choice.

> *So why do I hope that you will find this book at least a little bit stupid? Because it's my opinion.*

I have some favorite authors whom I think are brilliant. I have learned a lot from them. But if they told me how to go live *my* individual life, or gave me some advice and didn't ask me to think for myself first, I would probably be annoyed. My reaction would be, "Hey, dude, you can encourage me and give great information to me, but don't tell me how to *be*. Why would you want me to just listen to you instead of thinking for myself?" And that's probably why a conversation with my favorite authors might be awkward, and they would not ask for my contact information. You are a competent, smart, capable human being. Tap into that. You can decide if this book is stupid or if you agree with it. But please, be nice. I get sensitive.

Thinking and How It Could Be Good for Your Life

If I were Hester from *The Scarlet Letter*, I hope I would have the courage to hold my head high and not let past mistakes rob me of my dignity and my life. As I go through my life, I believe it's important to question how I am living. Am I doing the right thing? For myself? For others? For God? And when people share something with me in a talk or in a book, I try to take their words and thoughts into serious consideration. But I do so with a mind that evaluates the content of what they say and how it applies to my life.

Now you try it. Here is an example of what I mean. Consider this question:

Dear Chad,

There is this guy that I know, and he is always begging for attention. He is always cracking perverted jokes, and it gets annoying. I don't want to stop being around him, because he is a really good friend. What should I do? I don't know if I can take it much longer.

—Lizzy

Now, if this were you, what would *you* say to the guy? Would you need advice from someone else? Or, after thinking about it for a bit, could you actually decide for yourself what to do? Think about the obvious facts here:

Guy wants attention from anyone. (Probably something unhealthy happening there.)

Guy is being perverted and doesn't get that it's annoying to many people.

Guy is unaware that he is being disrespectful.

Guy is a good friend. (Really? Is he?)

I mean, it seems like there are three options here:

1. **Ignore the fact that his behavior bothers you.** Keep hanging around him. Keep being disrespected and annoyed, and never say a word to him—or to any other people who do that to you in life. Sounds like a great habit, right?

2. **Run away and never look back.** He is no longer your friend, and you avoid all contact with him. Never explain, just cut him out of your life completely. You know, the "cut-and-run" scenario. Except you will probably still see him in the hallways and at class and at lunch and at places around town, and therefore . . . this will be awkward.

3. **Or, if he really is your friend, you can simply tell him kindly, but firmly and clearly, that he is coming off as too attention–hungry.** You don't like his jokes, and you would like him to stop making them, at least around you. Is this more of a direct, sensible answer?

> Hey friend who's a part-time pervert who needs attention he isn't getting at home, please listen clearly. You are a friend, so you can listen to me, correct? I would appreciate it if you could just nix the pervert jokes. I can't be around you if you keep telling them. They aren't funny, and they make people feel uncomfortable and annoyed. This includes me. It's not healthy to act this way, and I care about you. So thanks for listening, and I hope you'll consider my words. Or we can't be friends, and I would like to be. Later, skater [or insert other catchy signoff here].

How would you answer when it's the other way around?

Chad,

I don't know if it's just my school or not, but girls act like huge teases, and it's like a game they play to get attention and mess with people, including me. There's a girl I like and have liked for a while. She uses me. She lets me take her places, and she will ask me to listen and to use my time and attention to talk about her problems. She says she likes me but she just can't be in a relationship right now. But she goes and hooks up with other guys and loves to flirt and get attention and has started dating someone who is a friend of mine. But she said last night she has feelings for me; it's just complicated. Girls are weird. What would you do?

—Brandon

You get the point, right? And these are no genius answers. You know that talking to someone first, and telling him or her clearly and kindly what the problem is, is the most obvious course of action for a reasonable person.

So maybe you don't need me, or people like me, as much as you think. I would take that as a compliment in some strange way. I mean, I think that you are a lot smarter and more capable than maybe you have been led to believe.

Here's some stuff to get you started:

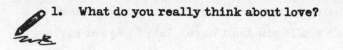

1.   What do you really think about love?

_____

_____

2.   Do you care about love a lot right now, a little, or not at all? How do you think you are expected to feel about love?

_____

_____

3.   What constitutes happiness?

_____

_____

4.   Do you really want to date? A lot? Or a little? Or you don't think about it? Why?

_____

_____

5. Is being "just friends" a bad thing to you? Does it matter to you if you don't have a lot of guys or girls wanting to date you? Why or why not?

_____

_____

6. If you were Hester Prynne, how would you react in her situation? (I mean, besides getting pregnant outside of your marriage. Obviously.)

_____

_____

I am hopeful for you. I hope that you will consciously choose your own path. I hope this book won't do anything but help you think for yourself. I hope you will choose to be competent; to question what people tell you; to ask yourself what you actually want from dating, what you think about friendship, how you want to love and be loved, and what you want in every other part of your life. It's ultimately your decision. But you must choose to decide for yourself. The only alternative is to let someone else decide for you. And that's no way to live . . . or to love.

14

LOTS OF OTHER IMPORTANT STUFF THAT WE'RE FINALLY GETTING TO LATER

I always thought the dishwasher was invented to make washing dishes easier. But although it does do that, that wasn't the reason it was created.

The first dishwasher was invented in 1886 by Josephine Garis Cochran of Illinois—though she did not even wash the dishes herself; her servants did. But Josephine got tired of her expensive china dishes being broken and chipped by the servants. So she finally got fed up and, with the help of an engineer friend, she designed the first dishwashing machine in a woodshed. The invention won first prize in 1893 at the Chicago World's Fair.[1]

Dishwashers and Dating ◀◀

So what do dishwashers have to do with dating? Funny you should ask. I thought about this story of the dishwasher because I was looking through pictures of a trip I took recently. I was in a place where there were no dishwashers, and not much of anything else either. I was lucky enough to take a trip to Rwanda, in Africa, to learn about a wonderful organization called World Vision and what they are doing there to help. In 1994, the country was torn to pieces by genocide, leaving countless children without a family. I expected to find heartache, but what I actually found was incredible. It was a place full of beauty, with beautiful people learning to heal and living full of love, even though they had experienced horrors that hopefully none of us ever will.

One day, with our big, goofy SUVs and video crew, we were far up in the mountains in the middle of nowhere, meeting people in small villages and looking at the countryside—which is tropical and breathtaking, with hints of cooking fires in the air and little goats running around in the grass, while boys and girls play soccer in any open clearing.

When we were visiting some victims of HIV and AIDS in a remote village, we crossed paths with a few young ladies. They were teenagers, and they were shy. But they were interested in what we were doing, as was everyone else, since they only saw white people about every six months or so. So we started talking with these young girls, who were between fifteen and sixteen. Through our translator, we asked them what it was like to be a teenage girl in Rwanda, just because we were curious. We asked them what they liked to do, if they were in school, what they did for fun, and then about boys, of course. And that's when the conversation changed.

I wanted to know how these Rwandan girls were like American girls, and how they might be different. I asked them what they found attractive in a guy. I asked them what they thought guys found attractive in them. I asked them what they thought it meant to feel beautiful. I mean, I know that they don't have TV or the Internet, but what they said was so unexpected I had to choke back my feelings.

After all that they had been through, those young girls told me that to them being attractive meant that they should have a humble heart, be caring toward others, have a good spirit, try to be educated, and take care of their hearts. They didn't have makeup, and they told me that they feel beauty comes from within themselves, and they can choose to see it or not. And I held in a tear. They weren't being proud, and they weren't telling me what they thought I wanted to hear.

Then they said that an attractive boy was someone who was kind and strong and cared about having a good heart and being a good man one day. I can't tell you what that moment was like, but I will say that I felt sobered by their words. Although they had practically nothing, they seemed more content—more content than I was. It was confusing.

Maybe we have a lot to learn from one another, especially when it comes to being friends, and loving, and relationships. Maybe those girls on the other side of the world aren't right about everything, but maybe we aren't right about a lot of things too.

Perhaps the key truth in all this is that, more than romance or love or dating, we need to have deep friendships, and we need to learn to be great friends in return. Perhaps we become miserable when we can't get what we want when we want it. And perhaps we need to have faith that patience does pay off. Maybe we have a lot to learn about putting relationships, and dating, and love in the appropriately sized containers in our heart. Maybe we can learn to control these emotions and desires instead of letting them control us.

"*Perhaps the key truth in all this is that, more than romance or love or dating, we need to have deep friendships, and we need to learn to be great friends in return.*"

To be honest, the truth about dating, love, just being friends, and all that other stuff is that there are many answers that can't be just simply given to you. For some questions, you will have to search and struggle for the truths and the wisdom and the answers that really matter. But it will be worth the journey. Yes, you will make mistakes along the way. I do all the time. But when you fall down seven times, just make sure you stand up eight.

*When you fall down seven times,
just make sure you stand up eight.*

If you get lost along the way, I hope you will look to good people to help you, and I hope you will look up to God. You are important, and so is your journey. This life is wonderful, and it is also really difficult, but it's still beautiful. I'll be here for you, hoping, and encouraging, and praying for you. These are your choices, and this is your heart; go and do good things with them.

*Today you are You,
that is truer than
true. There is no one
alive who is Youer
than you.*

—Dr. Seuss

NOTES

Chapter 1: What's Up, Milleys?

1.   S. J. J. F. Davies and B. C. R. Bertram, "Ostrich," in *Firefly Encyclopedia of Birds*, ed. Christopher Perrins (Buffalo, NY: Firefly Books, Ltd, 2003), 34–37; John Mitchinson and John Lloyd, *The Book of General Ignorance* (New York: Harmony Books, 2006), 144–45.

2.   Pew Research Center, "Millennials: Confident. Connected. Open to Change," February 24, 2010, http://pewsocialtrends.org/pubs/751/millennials-confident-connected-open-to-change.

3.   Ibid.

4.   Ibid.

5.   Amanda Lenhart, Mary Madden, and Paul Hitlin, "Teens and Technology," Pew Internet & American Life Project, July 27, 2005, http://www.pewinternet.org/~/media//Files Reports/2005/PIP_Teens_Tech_July2005web.pdf.

6.   See note 2 above.

7.   See note 2 above.

8.   Teen Help, "Teen Bulimia Statistics," 2010, http://www.teenhelp.com/eating-disorders/bulimia-statistics.html; Teen Help, "Teen Eating Disorder Statistics, 2010, http://www.teenhelp.com/eating-disorders/eating-disorder-statistics.html.

9.   M. H. Klein, J. H. Greist, and A. S. Gurman, "A Comparative Outcome Study of Group Psychotherapy vs. Exercise Treatments for Depression," *International Journal of Mental Health* 13 (1985): 148–77; Mayo Clinic Staff, "Depressions and Anxiety: Exercise Eases Symptoms," Mayo Foundation for Medical Education and Research, October 23, 2009, http://www.mayoclinic.com/health/depression-and-exercise/MH00043; Tommy Boone, "Benefits of Walking," http://health.howstuffworks.com/wellness/diet-fitness/exercise/benefits-of-walking6.htm.

10.   "U.S. Teen Sexual Activity," Kaiser Family Foundation, January 2005, http://www.kff.org/youthhivstds/upload/U-S-Teen-Sexual-Activity-Fact-Sheet.pdf.

11.   See note 2 above.

Chapter 2: Dating, Factoids, and Quark-Gluon Plasma

1.   John Mitchinson and John Lloyd, *The Book of General Ignorance*, (New York: Harmony Books, 2006), 89–90.

2.   Kimberly Powell, "Romance Through the Ages: Customs of Love, Marriage & Dating," http://genealogy.about.com/cs/timelines/a/romance_history.com.

3.   Ibid.

4.   Richard Daniel Altick, *Victorian People and Ideas: A Companion for the Modern Reader of Victorian Literature.* (New York: W. W. Norton & Company, 1974); Wikipedia, s.v. "Victorian Era," http://en.wikipedia.org/wiki/Victorian_era.

5.   See note 2 above.

6.   See note 2 above.

7.   Natasha Jackson-Arnautu, "History of Dating & Courtship," http://www.ehow.com/about_4570730_history-dating-courtship.html.

8.   Ibid.

9.   Dr. Henry Cloud and Dr. John Townsend, *Boundaries in Dating: Making Dating Work* (Grand Rapids, MI: Zondervan, 2000).

Chapter 3: Dumb Dating Mistakes—That Even Smart People Make

1. Andrew Thompson, *What Did We Use Before Toilet Paper?: 200 Curious Questions and Intriguing Answers* (Berkeley, CA: Ulysses Press, 2010), 74.
2. Bureau of Justice Special Report, "Intimate Partner Violence," May 2001, http://bjs.ojp .usdoj.gov/index.cfm?ty=tp&tid=971.
3. Ibid.
4. HelpGuide.Org, "Domestic Violence and Abuse: Signs of Abuse and Abusive Relationships," http://helpguide.org/mental/domestic_violence_abuse_types_signs_causes_ effects.htm; National Center for Victims of Crime, "Domestic Violence," http://www.ncvc.org/ ncvc/main.aspx?dbName=DocumentViewer&DocumentID=32347.
5. Ibid.
6. Ibid.
7. Ibid.

Chapter 4: What to Expect While You're Expecting—A Date

1. Andrew Thompson, *What Did We Use Before Toilet Paper?: 200 Curious Questions and Intriguing Answers* (Berkeley, CA: Ulysses Press, 2010), 205–7.

Chapter 5: Love and Other Chemical Imbalances

1. John Mitchinson and John Lloyd, *The Book of General Ignorance*, (New York: Harmony Books, 2006), 45–46.
2. Dr. Henry Cloud and Dr. John Townsend, *Boundaries in Dating: Making Dating Work* (Grand Rapids, MI: Zondervan, 2000), 129.
3. Jena Pincott, *Do Gentleman Really Prefer Blondes? Bodies, Behavior, and Brains. The Science Behind Sex, Love, & Attraction* (New York: Random House, 2008), 280–86; D. Marazziti and D. Canale, "Hormonal Changes When Falling in Love," *Psychoneuroendocrinology*, 29:7 (2004): 931– 36; Arthur Aron, Helen Fisher, Debra J. Mashek, Greg Strong, Haifang Li, and Lucy L. Brown, "Reward, Motivation, and Emotion Systems Associated with the Early-Stage Intense Romantic Love," *Journal of Neurophysiology*, 94, (July 2005): 327–37; J. Simao and P. M. Todd, "Emergent Patterns of Mate Choice in Human Populations," *Artificial Life*, 9 (Fall 2003): 403–17.; P. M. Todd, "Coevolved Cognitive Mechanisms in Mate Search: Making Decisions in a Decision-Shaped World," in *Evolution and the Social Mind: Evolutionary Psychology and Social Cognition*, eds. Joeseph P. Forgas, Martie G. Haselton, and William von Hippel (New York: Psychology Press, 2007), 147–58.
4. Rick Warren, *The Purpose Driven Life* (Grand Rapids, MI: Zondervan, 2002).

Chapter 6: Just Friends!?!

1. John Mitchinson and John Lloyd, *The Book of General Ignorance* (New York: Harmony Books, 2006), 96–99.
2. Dictionary.com, s.v. "Friendship," http://dictionary.reference.com/browse/friendship; Merriam-Webster Dictionary Online, s.v. "Friendship," http://www.merriam-webster.com/ dictionary/friendship.
3. Lauren John, "Nurturing Your Baby's Brain," July–August 2001, http://www.4children .org; U.S. Department of Health and Human Services, "Child Maltreatment," 2007, http://www .acf.hhs.gov/programs/cb/pubs/cm07/chapter3.htm#sex.
4. Dr. Henry Cloud and Dr. John Townsend, *Boundaries in Dating: Making Dating Work* (Grand Rapids, MI: Zondervan, 2000), 116–30.

Chapter 7: What Do They Want, Anyway?

1. John Mitchinson and John Lloyd, *The Book of General Ignorance* (New York: Harmony Books, 2006), 74–75.
2. Myers-Briggs Test, http://www.myersbriggsreports.com; DISC Personality Test, http://www.thediscpersonalitytest.com; Marcus Buckingham, *Now, Discover Your Strengths* (New York: Free Press, 2001).

Chapter 8: Crazy, Dumb, and Mixed-Up Feelings

1. E. K. Miller and J. D. Cohen, "Integrative Theory of Prefrontal Cortex Function," *Annual Review of Neuroscience* 24 (2001): 167–202; http://arjournals.annualreviews.org/doi/abs/10.1146%2Fannurev.
2. Bill and Pam Farrel, *Men Are Like Waffles—Women Are Like Spaghetti* (Eugene, OR: Harvest House, 2001), 189–90; E. K. Miller and J. D. Cohen, "Integrative Theory of Prefrontal Cortex Function," *Annual Review of Neuroscience* 24 (2001): 167–202; Daniel Goleman, *Emotional Intelligence: Why It Can Matter More Than IQ* (New York: Bantam, 1995).
3. John Gottman, *The Mathematics of Marriage* (Cambridge, MA: MIT Press, 2003); John M. Gottman, *Why Marriages Succeed or Fail* (New York: Simon & Schuster, 1994).
4. Holli Marshall, "The Feelings Chart," http://www.healthyplace.com/abuse/hollis-triumph-over-tragedy/the-feelings-chart/menu-id-1890/.
5. John C. Friel and Linda D. Friel, *The 7 Best Things (Smart) Teens Do* (Deerfield Beach, FL: Health Communications, 2000), 59–82, 211–22.

Chapter 9: Miserable Teenagers

1. Andrew Thompson, *What Did We Use Before Toilet Paper?: 200 Curious Questions and Intriguing Answers* (Berkeley, CA: Ulysses Press, 2010), 87–88; John Mitchinson and John Lloyd, *The Book of General Ignorance* (New York: Harmony Books, 2006), 217–18; *QI: The Complete First Series - QI Factoids*, DVD, directed by Ian Lorimer (London: 2 entertain Ltd, 2006); Clark Heinrich, *Magic Mushrooms in Religion and Alchemy* (Rochester, NY: Park Street Press, 2002), 64–70.
2. C. S. Lewis, *The Great Divorce* (San Francisco: HarperOne, 2009).

Chapter 10: Happy Teenagers

1. John Mitchinson and John Lloyd, *The Book of General Ignorance* (New York: Harmony Books, 2006), 117–18.
2. "How to Make a Teenager Happy," http://www.ehow.com/how_4807210_teenager-happy.html#ixzz0yClspNql.
3. Dr. Martin Seligman, *Authentic Happiness: Using the New Positive Psychology to Realize Your Potential for Lasting Fulfillment* (New York: Free Press, 2002).
4. Ibid.
5. Chad Eastham, *Guys Are Waffles, Girls Are Spaghetti* (Nashville, TN: Thomas Nelson, 2009); Chad Eastham, *The Truth About Guys* (Nashville, TN: Thomas Nelson, 2006).

Chapter 11: It's Not Okay to Be Dumb

1. John Mitchinson and John Lloyd, *The Book of General Ignorance* (New York: Harmony Books, 2006), 37–39.

2.   Wikipedia, s.v. "Competence (biology)," http://en.wikipedia.org/wiki/Competence_
(biology).

3.   Malcolm Gladwell, *Outliers: The Story of Success* (New York: Little, Brown and Company,
2008), 69–115; John C. Friel and Linda D. Friel, *The 7 Best Things (Smart) Teens Do* (Deerfield
Beach, FL: Health Communications, 2000), 37–59.

Chapter 12: The Problem with Falling in Love with Mythical Creatures

1.   Andrew Thompson, *What Did We Use Before Toilet Paper?: 200 Curious Questions and
Intriguing Answers* (Berkeley, CA: Ulysses Press, 2010), 34–35; Leonardo Vitini, "Ngoc Thai: The
Man Who Doesn't Sleep," *The Epoch Times*, October 8, 2010, http://www.theepochtimes.com/
n2/content/view/2855/; What's the Latest, "Thai Ngoc—The Man Who Doesn't Sleep, 2009,
http://www.whatsthelatest.net/for-the-records/thai-ngoc-man-sleep/.

2.   Matthew Inman, "How Twilight Works," http://theoatmeal.com/story/twilight.

Chapter 13: Why This Book Could Be Stupid

1.   John Mitchinson and John Lloyd, *The Book of General Ignorance* (New York: Harmony
Books, 2006), 8–9.

Chapter 14: Lots of Other Important Stuff, That We're Finally Getting to Later

1.   John Mitchinson and John Lloyd, *The Book of General Ignorance* (New York: Harmony
Books, 2006), 183–84.